READING THROUGH
GENESIS

WITH
THE DEVOTED COLLECTIVE

The Devoted Collective
Auckland, New Zealand
www.thedevotedcollective.org

ISBN Hardcover 978-0-473-61373-0

Cover design by Holly Robertson of Design by Rocket www.designbyrocket.com
Book Illustrations by Marie Warner Preston of Outspoken Images www.outspokenimages.com
Edited by Ellie Di Julio and Aimée Walker

Cataloguing in Publishing Data Title: Reading Through Genesis
Author: The Devoted Collective
Subjects: Devotions, Christian life, Spirituality

A copy of this title is held at the National Library of New Zealand

In the beginning...

The Bible opens with a story of community; Father, Son, and Holy Spirit labouring together in perfect unity to create something beautiful. It's a theme established in Genesis that will echo throughout the pages of Scripture: God does not work in isolation. He operates in community, continually widening the circle as He invites us to join Him in His work. And just as each member of the Trinity plays a distinct role in that work, so do we each bring our different giftings to building the Kingdom.

In this book, we invite you to read through Genesis with this same sense of community, enjoying the unique perspectives and experiences that the different members of our writing team bring to this familiar text. Each day, you'll read a portion of Scripture paired with a devotion designed to help you sink deep into the Word to reflect on God's goodness, mercy, sovereignty, and love that has been on display from the first moment of Creation.

It is our prayer that these words enrich your understanding of His Word, strengthening your relationship with the One who has loved you from the start of it all and helping you to step into the part He is calling you to play in the unfolding of that story today.

The Devoted Team

Contents

Functional Purpose

ELLIE DI JULIO

Genesis 1:1-23

I am currently the proud owner of a non-existent house. Oh, you can locate it on a map—you can even go inside. But when you do, you'll find walls and floors ripped up, air ducts missing, and water and electricity shut off. It's totally uninhabitable. It doesn't serve the purpose of a house (yet), so functionally, it doesn't exist.

This example sounds silly to a modern mind, which equates existence to physical matter, but to the audience for whom Genesis was originally written, functionality was their focus: *Does a thing serve a purpose? Who or what is it serving?* If a thing did not have a clear purpose, then it had no bearing on reality. For these ancient Hebrews, the *who* and *why* of Creation was more important than the *how*.

When we look at the days outlined in Genesis 1 through this lens of function rather than form, a pattern of purpose begins to emerge. First, God speaks the division of time (vv.3-5), the formation of weather (vv.6-8), and the establishment of food (vv.7-13). He then populates Creation with heavenly bodies (vv.14-19), sea creatures and birds (vv.20-23), and land animals (vv.24-25).

This is truly awesome. No mortal being could create order from chaos this way. But the lingering question is *why?* God is perfect; He has no needs. If for a thing to exist in the ancient Hebrew conception it must serve a purpose, whose needs will be served when Creation is finished?

We find our answer in the sixth day as humanity is given its own purpose: to rule and reign as the very image of God (vv.26-27). Each day of Creation, each thing God speaks into being finds its purpose in service of mankind. By establishing time, weather, food, and a dominion to rule, the needs of humans are met.

Yet a further question remains. Creation's function is fulfilled in service to humanity, but what is the divine function of humans? *How do we know who and why we are?*

Through Christ.

In our materialistic modern culture, it's easy to focus on the form of our existence—our house, job, family, church—and feel like we serve what is intended to serve us. We forget our function, our aching soul spiralling into existential crisis. It is only through turning our focus ever back to Jesus that we can hope to be restored to our original purpose.

Unnamed yet all-important, Jesus is present in the beginning. He is the Word God speaks to imbue the material of Creation with purpose (John 1:1; Genesis 1:3-31), the One through and for whom all things were created (Colossians 1:16). Though He has no needs, He desired to create us for relationship with Him—and that was enough.

And He continues to desire us. It would have been just for God to discard humanity once we became dysfunctional, His image in us marred after the Fall into sin. But because of His unfailing love and mercy, Jesus shed His blood to rescue us from that death, that non-existence, and restore us to life and purpose (Ephesians 2:13).

In the beginning, God created the heavens and the earth (Genesis 1:1), purposing them to serve humanity and for humanity to be in relationship with Him. Through the salvation of Christ, present in the first breath of Creation, we are restored to our original function, able to truly image God and to reign with Him. Before time began, Jesus bestowed on us our true purpose as divine image bearers, and He continues to uphold it in the moments when we forget who we are and why we're here, ever willing to remind us as we continue to put our faith in Him.

For our good and His glory—since day one.

Take a moment to brainstorm all the words that spring to mind when you think about 'purpose.' Now consider how these align with your God-given purpose of reflecting Christ and reigning with Him and through Him. Are there any changes you need to make in your thinking or habits to better enable you to fulfil your original function?

In His Image

PAULA MORRISON

Genesis 1:24-2:3

Occasionally I watch a TV show called *Lost and Found* where adopted children look for their birth parents. They're driven by a deep need to know their origins and to find the answers to their questions: *Who do they belong to? Who do they look like?* When they do meet their birth family for the first time and finally have the answers they've been desperately searching for, I always cry. I see reflected in their stories my own quest for identity and belonging.

Genesis is a book of origins, and in the opening chapter we find the answer to our own questions: We are made in the image of God (1:26). He is the One we are called to resemble and the One we belong to.

It is humans alone who are like God and who are given authority over all other created things. Unlike the rest of creation, humans are spiritual beings, set apart and made for a relationship with God. Both male and female image bearers are equal and necessary for the image of God to be demonstrated to the world; both are blessed by Him (1:27-28), giving every person significance and intrinsic value. As we lean into this truth, spending time with Him and growing in maturity, our family resemblance to Him becomes unmistakable.

My own questions of identity and belonging have led to me asking, *What is my purpose in life?* It follows that if we are created in the image of God, then there has to be a divine purpose for our existence. Again, we find our answer in the pages of Genesis: "'Be fruitful and increase in number; fill the earth and subdue it'" (1:28). This mandate applies both physically and spiritually. God's people are called to populate the earth so that the Gospel can bear fruit and grow throughout the whole world (Colossians 1:6). It's our life's work to share the good news—news that will lead others to the truth of their origin where they will find their identity in God and belonging in His family.

But this mandate is not solely fulfilled through our work; it is also perpetuated through rest. By the seventh day, God has finished His act of creation and rests from all work. As we are like God, we, too, flourish when we have a regular rhythm of rest. Practically, this will look different for each of us, but in our world of hustle, God teaches us to stop work, know our limits, and worship Him alone (Exodus 20:8). Just as God rests in His finished work of Creation, we today rest in the finished work of Christ. We are no longer slaves to sin (Romans 6:6) but can enjoy the presence of God with the unhurried comfort of a loving family gathering.

It seems incomprehensible to me that the God of the universe created me to be like Him, inviting me to know Him and bring Him glory through my life. Today, if you feel you don't have value or don't belong, remember that God created you in His image to be part of His family. You are not an accident, and your life is imbued with divine purpose. You can live each day secure in the truth of your origin, knowing who you belong to and who you are like.

Spend some time asking the Holy Spirit to show you the specific and unique ways in which you resemble the Father. Thank Him for the fearful and wonderful way He has made you, and consider how He is inviting you to use these gifts and qualities to share the Good News.

DAY THREE

A Suitable Helper
AMBER PALMER

Genesis 2:4-25

As the words, *"I do,"* came from my mouth, I couldn't help but feel complete as I held my new husband's hand in my own. After years of walking on this earth alone, waiting for 'the one,' God had blessed me with a soulmate to call mine. A peace came over me knowing I was never going to be alone again. I would always have a companion to do life with—a forever helper, someone I could lean on and trust.

When God brought Adam to life from mere dust, He knew Adam shouldn't be alone. The animals that roamed around the earth and in the sky wouldn't make the best companions; he needed a "helper fit for him" (2:18 ESV). I have read these words many times before, but this go-round they held a bigger picture, an *aha* moment I couldn't shake. When I read aloud the word 'helper,' the words of the Holy Spirit filled my heart. God knew not even Adam's helper, Eve, would complete him in every way or be everything he needed. As Moses scribed the word 'helper,' *ezer*, meaning God's strength, protection, help and rescuing, God was already looking ahead to Jesus and the gift of the Holy Spirit, our ultimate Helper.

In John 14:26, Jesus shares with His disciples, "'But the Helper, the Holy Spirit, whom the Father will send in my name, He will teach you all things, and remind you of all that I said to you'" (NASB). The Greek word for 'Helper' in this verse, *parakletos*, means 'one who is called to one's side, especially to help.' It is used to describe someone who intercedes and advocates on behalf of another, one who consoles and comforts. The Holy Spirit provides the best helpmeet. He is a helper perfectly fit for you and me. The most beautiful part is that He comes not only to dwell with us, but also *within* us so we can always be together. Just as God did in the Garden of Eden, He made a way so we would never have to be alone again.

It was wishful thinking on the part of my young newlywed heart to think one person alone could complete and fulfil me in every way. No human relationship can do that. While we are designed for and must pursue community, the reality is we will fail each other one way or another. We will all fall short and mess up. Sometimes we are part of the pain others experience on this side of Heaven as we sift through our own selfish desires;

other times we are on the receiving end and find ourselves disappointed when expectations are not met or our minds are not read. The pain of feeling alone, hurt, and unworthy can be too much to endure at times.

I'm grateful God foresaw the brokenness of our human relationships and provided the best helper of all, the Holy Spirit. He will never let us down, turn His back on us, or deem us not good enough to love. Rather, He will always champion us, deepen our faith, provide protection, bring comfort, and strengthen us for whatever comes our way so that our lives can bear the fruit God intended. In Him, we have been blessed with a true and lasting gift from God; He is the suitable helper our hearts have been longing for.

Where in your life are you looking to people to meet a need that only God can fulfil? What might it look like for you to turn to the Holy Spirit for help in that place today?

Modern-Day Eves

JENNA MARIE MASTERS

Genesis 3

The phone rings, and I brace myself. It's just the eye doctor. I send the call to voicemail and surrender to tears.

Please, Father. Give me answers.

It's court day. I'm waiting to hear if our foster daughter will stay with us for six more months or if she'll go back to her biological mother.

God, please. You know. Why won't you just tell me everything so I can have peace?!

And just like that, I was a modern-day Eve—desiring answers more than I desired my Abba Father in Heaven. I had convinced myself I could find peace outside of His glorious presence.

Eve had the honour of walking in the cool of the evening with her Father God. She had unimaginable intimacy with the craftsman of her soul. Yet when she was offered the chance to know more—*more than the presence of God*—she bit.

Eve trades intimacy for information. It is a devastating mistake. She gains knowledge of good and evil, yet the first thing she does is confuse the two. She covers up her nakedness, acting as if what God planned and declared 'good' is shameful.

Soon after, the Lord looks for Eve and her husband in the garden. God knows she needs peace, and only His presence can provide it. But now that their sin has left them exposed, they are afraid of the very One they once delighted in, and so they "hid themselves from the presence of the Lord among the trees of the garden" (Genesis 3:8 NASB). When God finds them, He asks, "'Who told you that you were naked?'" (v.11). In other words, "*Who told you something is wrong with what I've planned for your life? Who said what I've provided isn't enough?*"

We do the same thing. When we need God's peace the most, we often question His purposes and run from Him. Sometimes we flee in anger, sometimes in shame, sometimes dragging grief or fear of the unknown. The trouble is, the moment we pull ourselves from the presence of the Lord, anxiety rises and we do crazy things. Adam and Eve sew clothes out of fig leaves thinking they have the power to cover themselves in peace; I spend vast amounts of time and energy seeking answers on Facebook and texting veteran foster mamas on court days. We search for answers elsewhere, looking for someone to help us stitch together what we think the Lord won't. What we communicate to God through this behaviour is that we would rather know God's plans than know *Him*. But if we believe Scripture is true, then we already know God's plans for us: good plans to prosper and not to harm us, plans to give us hope and a future (Jeremiah 29:11).

So when the serpent whispers devious words in my ear—"*Did God really say that?*"—I will think of my sister Eve and remember that God is not withholding delicious fruits from me because He's a careless Father; He is a kind Father who knows what is best for me. I will remember how, even when God's daughter didn't trust His word, when she hid in shame, separated from His presence, God still had a plan.

And His plan was good.

God compassionately made the first sacrifice to cover His children's shame in garments of skin. But the covering was only temporary, for the Fall produced a curse of thorns (v.18). Thousands of years later, King Jesus, "becoming the curse for us," wore those thorns as a crown, suffered the final sacrifice, and rose from the grave—so we could walk in the garden with Him again (Galatians 3:13).

I remind myself of all of this as I turn my phone on silent, close my eyes, and pray: "Father God, help me to pursue Your presence over understanding Your purposes. I want to walk with You, Abba, more than I want answers."

Where in your life have you been trading information for intimacy? What would it look like for you to relinquish control and connect your heart to the Father's?

DAY FIVE

Invisible Chains

AIMÉE WALKER

Genesis 4

It's a familiar story: Two brothers bring their offerings before the Lord—
one is accepted, one isn't. Consequently, the brothers have a fall-out of epic
proportions and history has its first murderer. And a defiant one at that!
When God asks Cain where his brother is, despite knowing full-well where
Abel lies, he replies, "I don't know. Am I my brother's keeper?" (Genesis
4:9).

*What would make a man spiral from jealousy into a rage so deep he would take
his brother's life?*

In a word: Pride.

The original language of Genesis 4 conveys that there is a fixed time and
way in which offerings are to be made. In other words, Cain knows what is
required of him. He knows that acceptable offerings must come from the
'firstfruits' *and* involve the shedding of blood—anything less is powerless to
cover sin. And yet, he ignores all of this, choosing instead to approach God
on his own terms and bring an offering of leftovers grown from the cursed
soil. When it is rejected, his anger blooms.

It seems the height of arrogance to ignore the instructions of God Himself
and rely on your own efforts. But if I'm honest, I've been Cain many a time.
I've been him every time I've tried to earn God's favour, every time I've
fallen into striving and rule-keeping and list-ticking, every time I've relied
on my own goodness or gone my own way. Pride is the invisible chain that
for many years kept me from truly experiencing grace.

And it's this same chain that enslaves Cain. But he doesn't have to *stay*
stuck in his pride.

God graciously offers Cain a way to master the sin seeking to control him
by drawing near and inviting him to do what is right and offer a proper
sacrifice. But again, Cain chooses his own path. It's not until he has to carry
the full weight of his sin against his brother that he realises what he has
lost: He will be hidden from God's presence, and it is more than he can
bear.

Doomed to be a restless wanderer, Cain is afraid that outside of God's protection, whoever finds him will kill him (vv.13-14). And God is merciful. Despite Cain's unrepentant heart and unwillingness to offer the necessary sacrifice to atone for his sin, God offers him grace. Cain must bear the consequences of his actions, but God assuages his fear of death by extending to him a seal of protection.

Once again, I realise how like Cain I can be. Fear often lies at the root of my own pride and anger—the fear of failing, of not being good enough, of being rejected and alone. This fear is why the Cross has often been a stumbling block to me: It forces me to confront my deepest fears and failings and demands that I accept I have fallen short.

I, too, need God's grace. And thankfully, God has generously given it.

Abel, a simple shepherd, by faith offered God an acceptable sacrifice, and though not by choice, his blood was shed, foreshadowing the ultimate Shepherd, Jesus, whose blood speaks a better word than Abel's (Hebrews 12:24). The firstborn of all Creation (Colossians 1:15), He is the unblemished offering that, when humbly accepted, washes us clean and enables us to once again draw near to God (Hebrews 9:14, 10:21-22).

We need not fear death or wander alone any longer. When we exercise faith in the finished work of the Cross, the mark that we bear—the mark that enables us to live free from fear—is that of the Holy Spirit. He is the seal upon our lives (Ephesians 1) and the One that enables us to daily master sin and walk in the fullness of all that Jesus, our Good Shepherd, laid His life down for us to possess.

Where in your life do you see pride enslaving you? Ask the Holy Spirit to show you what fear is at the root of this pride and to minister to you the perfect love that casts out fear.

EMILY TYLER

Genesis 5

When enrolled in Deaf Studies at university, I was assigned a sign name by the Deaf community. It isn't simply 'Emily' spelt out but is actually the sign for 'crossed legs.' I was given this name because it reflected the fact that during my lectures, being short in stature, I would sit with both legs up on the chair and crossed underneath me. My sign name called out the truth about who I was as a person.

In the Deaf community, you don't get to choose your own name. Rather, you are observed over time, and eventually, an 'elder' of the community will assign one to you. This might be something about your physical appearance or about your character. A name from the Deaf community is so much more than a sign: It is an identifier of who you are at the core, and it's something owned by the community more than the individual.

Similarly, names in the Bible often prophetically call out significant details about the individual or community into which the child is born; they have a message and a meaning. We see this idea in Isaiah 62 (*no longer will you be called A, but instead you'll be called B*), Hosea 1, the naming of John the Baptist (Luke 1:59-66), and a whole host of other places.

Because a name is never just a name for God. Rich with symbolism and Hebrew literary practices, Old Testament genealogies have multiple layers of information simultaneously working to communicate God's big story, and Genesis 5 is no different. Together, these names paint a clear picture that, despite the events of chapter 4, the fall of humanity in chapter 3, and the apparent failure of His perfect world, God has not forgotten His people and has a beautiful plan for redemption.

Looking at the Hebrew meanings (in italics) of the names listed in this chapter, we can see the whole story of the Bible foreshadowed from Adam to Noah:

Humanity [Adam] needed an *appointed substitute* [Seth] to account for their *mortality* and sin [Enosh], which resulted in *lament* at the consequences of *finite* life on this earth (*dwelling*) [Kenan]. But *praise* be to our *strong* God [Mahalalel], who *descended* and *came down* [Jared] to *teach* and *train* up [Enoch] the people. He would be a *branch, a shoot, forsaken* and *pierced* [Methuselah], *humbled* and *lowered to death* [Lamech] that He might bring *rest* and *comfort* [Noah] for all.

From the beginning, God is remembering His people, planning for their redemption, and making a way for salvation and freedom to reign. I don't know about you, but I'll be less inclined to skip past genealogies after discovering the depth and meaning hidden within Genesis 5!

While in the Deaf community your name signifies one truth about you, when God names and calls you, nothing is left out. Under the banner of Christ's name, you are a new creation (2 Corinthians 5:17), a child of God (Galatians 3:26), free from condemnation (Romans 8:1), created for good works (Ephesians 2:10), one body (Romans 12:5), justified (Galatians 2:16), alive (1 Corinthians 1:30), triumphant (2 Corinthians 2:14), and blessed with every spiritual blessing (Ephesians 1:3)! There's redemption, grace, and intimacy: Before you were even born God knew you (Jeremiah 1:5), and He knows and calls you by name (Isaiah 43:1, Psalm 91:14, Exodus 33:17). Because of the shoot of Jesse who came down and died to bring you ultimate comfort, you can know, even today, the freedom of what it truly means to be called and named in Christ.

Your individual name says a lot about you, but God calls you to an even greater identity as part of the community of believers. Ask the Holy Spirit to reveal how you contribute to the unfolding of God's grand story and what you can do to further His Kingdom on earth today.

Noah's Righteousness

SHELLEY JOHNSON

Genesis 6

A few years ago, I made a choice to stop watching the nightly news. Its stories of bloodshed and brutality filled me with a dread that tried to convince me the world is hopeless because it is so evil. The inundation of negative news left me fearful, but I have discovered that when I look beyond the bad, I find families adopting orphans, strangers paying others' debts, and neighbours helping neighbours. There is still good in the world; it isn't only evil.

That was not the case in Noah's day. Genesis 6 opens with what seems a fulfilment of God's blessing to go forth and multiply, but these "sons of God" have twisted the good gifts He gave them and become tainted by the evil ways of unbelievers. Their mixed marriages and lustful eyes have led them into debauchery and violence. Verse five says plainly of the human race that "every inclination of the thoughts of the human heart was only evil all the time."

Only evil. All the time.

Not a few outliers. Not a particular group. We're talking about the entirety of humanity. All people, continually nurturing evil in their hearts and minds. Every single person. Every moment of every day.

This is the context for God's decision to flood the earth. As He looks down on all those He's created and watches them fall to the temptations of evil, He is grieved. His heart fills with the kind of pain only a much-beloved child can inflict on a devoted parent, a hurt so deep and fundamental that He is sorry to have made them.

In His just and holy way, God readies His hand for judgment because He sees no good.

But Noah.

This one man has continued to live for God when all of humanity has forsaken Him. Described as both 'righteous,' *tzaddik,* and 'perfect,' *tamim,* the Hebrew conveys the idea that both his heart *and* his actions are right before God, and it is because of this that Noah is called to be the curator during the cleansing of creation. God promises to covenant with this one man to reestablish the world as He'd intended it in the beginning—and in response, Noah does everything just as God commands. Noah steps into faithful obedience, trusting the Creator to recreate on the other side of disaster.

Hebrews 11:7 tells us that "by faith Noah, when warned about things not yet seen, in holy fear built an ark to save his family. By his faith he condemned the world and became heir of the righteousness that is in keeping with faith." Noah's faith and righteousness in the midst of a world intent on evil is a model for us to follow after, but ultimately, his life points us to Jesus. Through his obedience, Noah establishes himself as an early pattern of the Messiah, a foreshadowing of Christ, the One who came to rescue us from the darkness of sin and recreate us in His image.

As evil as our world often seems, it is not given over to only evil all the time. Good can be found, as can people who remain faithful to God, which means we can look to Noah and then to Jesus to find hope for our lives and a way forward in them. Each time we choose to trust God's way over the world's, we're stepping into a righteousness that we've been gifted through Christ's perfection and sacrifice on our behalf (Romans 5:17). It's by that righteous way of living that we can become vessels for God's grace to flow on the earth.

How is God inviting you to be obedient in this season?
What step could you take today to be faithful to what
He has said?

Hidden Seasons

RACHEL LOUISE

Genesis 7

With the concluding words of Genesis 7, we are left in an uncomfortable space. The waters have risen for over a hundred days (v.24). The face of the earth has been wiped bare. There isn't a single thing on the horizon, least of all hope.

It's a feeling we know well. When grief seems as if it will never abate, when sleep evades us, when bodies break down. It's the deep sorrow and hopelessness we meet on Good Friday. All is thrown into darkness without a glimmer of dawn. Christ our Saviour is buried in the grave and all seems lost.

Despite knowing this well-trodden narrative, despite knowing doves and olive branches and rainbows, sitting in this discomfort is important—because it leads us straight to the Cross. Before new life springs up, we struggle. Before resurrection, we lament. But even in the midst of the devastating deluge, we invariably land on glimpses of God's grace.

The Flood is a mighty display of God's immense power, unleashing "the springs of the great deep" and "the floodgates of the heavens" upon the earth (v.11-12). This is a God to be rightly feared. This is a God capable of throwing all existence into oblivion.

And yet, He doesn't. Right alongside utter destruction, God tenderly preserves life.

We see God's grace in His gentle invitation to Noah to "come into the ark" (v.1 KJV). The Lord beckons rather than sends Noah into a place of refuge. Obeying God's instruction, Noah has carved a space the waters cannot touch, and God is already there as he enters.

We see God's grace again in His seal of safety. The Lord shuts Noah in the ark Himself, holding Noah's protection in His hands alone (v.16). No matter the magnitude of disaster on the earth, life on the ark, in God's will, is a different story. We're told that "the ark floated on the surface" and "rose greatly" (v.18-19). Noah is shut away, yet uplifted and cared for beyond the destruction.

There are times when being hidden is the best thing for us.

My own shut-away season came after a series of devastating losses, as I sensed God was calling me somewhere new. I moved to the opposite side of the city and embarked on a nine-month formational theology course. While entering a new community set in a beautiful landscape offered something of a retreat from the wider world, life as I had known it was simultaneously unravelling in almost every way. But obedience lifted me above the floodwaters, giving me a gracious sense of distance from it all. I was safely hidden away for a richly life-giving season, and I felt God fiercely whisper that I would not be bowled over. There, I had perspective to see that the deluge wouldn't last forever.

God's grace is present even in circumstances that at first appear hopeless. When God sets the waters free from their restrictions, the destruction is bounded; it has a time limit. Just as He does not allow the waters into the ark, He does not allow them to rise beyond one hundred and fifty days (v.24). Even the mighty Flood is constrained.

And here, for us, the depth of our lament only increases the breadth of His mercy.

We follow a God of mighty power and gentle grace, characteristics that aren't contradictions but are resolved in the person of Jesus. For Christ is the Lion *and* the Lamb, capable of fearsome violence, yet willing to die so we may live. And because of this sacrifice, God's immense power is *for* us.

As the deluge pours in and out of our lives, with its current set against us, we hold onto the hope that God is *more* powerful. He is raising the very protection we need from incessant rains. We need only follow His beckoning as they begin to fall.

Recollect a moment when destruction seemed to be all around but God offered unexpected safety. Now consider where Christ might be inviting you to take refuge in Him today. What does it look like to respond to that invitation, propelled by His past faithfulness?

God Remembers

EMILY TYLER

Genesis 8

After the advent of COVID-19, we're no strangers to lockdowns: restrictions on movement, only seeing those you live with, comforts of life removed—we're beginning to relate to Noah in ways we perhaps hadn't before.

Reading this chapter, I'm struck by the vast amount of time Noah has to wait after the rain stops. We often think it rained for forty days and nights and then everyone left the ark straight away. In and out. Except that's not how it went down.

God tells Noah that he is going into the ark and for how long the rain will fall. What He doesn't say is how long Noah will be trapped inside after the rain ends. There is no mention of the days that turn into weeks and months of lockdown. Just the daily chaos of the ark's inhabitants and silence from God. I wouldn't be surprised if Noah began to feel forgotten. Everything appears lost. The world as he knew it has literally disappeared, and he's stuck in a floating prison. All he can hold onto is the promise God made to keep him alive (Genesis 6:20).

I love how even the structure of the Hebrew text helps us to focus on what is truly important. In Genesis 7 and 8, we see a palistrophe (an inversion of statements, e.g. ABCCBA) at play; the events of the rains coming and falling through chapter 7 are reversed through chapter 8 as the waters recede and Noah and his family can leave the ark. It's most easily seen in the days mentioned: 7, 7, 40, 150, 150, 40, 7, 7. The significance of this palistrophe hinges on the central turning point between the first and second 150 days. So what is this critical moment that provides a glimmer of hope that freedom is on its way?

"But God remembered Noah" (Genesis 8:1).

The Hebrew for 'remembered' in this verse is *zakar*, 'remembering that leads to action.' When we read that God remembers Noah, Rachel (Genesis 30:22), Sarah (Genesis 21:2), Abraham (Genesis 19:29), and many others, we can know change is coming—conception, answered prayer, rescue, or salvation. God remembers, then He moves.

Throughout the Bible, we're shown that God is in the business of remembering His people. He is mindful of us (Psalm 8), even if others forget or leave us, He will not (Isaiah 49:14-15). If He remembers the sparrows, then He's certainly going to remember you, infinitely precious you, and the situation you find yourself in (Luke 12:6-7).

The pinnacle of this narrative, the moment everything changes from bad to good, is God. *But God.* When we find ourselves in messy, dark, and long seasons of waiting, we must hold onto and remember God's promises. *But God* is still with us and acting on our behalf. No matter how forgotten we might feel, God *will* do what He has said (1 Thessalonians 5:24), and remembering who He is and what He has done awakens us to the comfort of His presence, taking us from a place of desperation to one of joy, hope, faith, and praise (Psalm 77).

The very crux of our faith centres on remembering that our future was changed from bad to good when Jesus endured the cross. No longer are we confined and imprisoned by sin because Jesus remembered you and then chose to act. He suffered the ultimate prison of death so that we could be brought out, like Noah, to receive new life—full of freedom, fruitfulness, and hope.

Whatever you're waiting for, remember this: God remembered Noah, and Jesus remembers you.

Reflect on the past week. In what ways has God shown you He is mindful of you? Take some time to give thanks for His faithful care and allow it to fuel an expectation for what is yet to be fulfilled in your life.

Written in the Skies

AIMÉE WALKER

Genesis 9

My husband used to joke that I had the memory of an elephant. My ability to recall the smallest of details from years back drove him mad (and meant he seldom won an argument). However, these days my memory feels a little frayed around the edges, and my son has taken to saying to me, "Remember?!" whenever he's concerned I'm going to forget a promise I've made to him.

God, on the other hand, has no such problem. One of the very first things He reveals about Himself in Scripture is that He is not a God who forgets, but a God who keeps His promises—a God who remembers.

In Genesis 9, God formally establishes the covenant He had promised Noah prior to the Flood (Genesis 6:18). Known as the Noahic Covenant, it is the first explicit covenant made by God with man, and like the Abrahamic Covenant, it is unconditional. In other words, its fulfilment is not dependent upon our performance but upon God's grace and mercy; He assumes full responsibility for its execution.

Within this covenant, we see echoes of the Creation story and the redemptive heart of God as He works to ensure that His original purposes for humanity are realised. Like He did for Adam, God blesses Noah and his sons, commanding them to be fruitful and replenish the earth, assuring them that they need not fear extinction again. As God's image-bearers, human life is sacred and must be protected. And so not only does God put a dread of mankind into the animal kingdom, vowing to hold to account every animal and man responsible for the shedding of human blood (vv.2-5), He also makes a commitment that "never again will there be a flood to destroy the earth" (v.11).

As a sign of this promise, God says He will "set His rainbow (*qesheth*) in the clouds" (v.13). A *qesheth* is a warrior's bow. God has hung His weapon in the sky as a symbol of His grace toward mankind; though the world might deserve destruction, He is instead allowing time for all to come to repentance (2 Peter 3:9). But the rainbow is also a symbol of His glory. Outside of Genesis, it is associated with the Shekinah Glory of God—His manifest presence (Ezekiel 1:28; Revelation 4:3), and as a refraction of pure white light, it speaks to His holiness and absolute perfection.

After establishing this covenant, twice within three verses, God says, "I will remember my covenant" (vv.14 & 16)—and we know that when God repeats Himself, it's time to pay attention! He's telling us, "Not only am I a promise-making God, but I am also a promise-*keeping* one." It's important to understand that when God says He will remember, He's not saying that He needs to be reminded lest He forget—the way we do. The language He uses is covenantal and conveys the idea of movement toward an object. It is an active word. God is making a statement about His commitment to be faithful to what He has promised. He cannot and will not forget what He has said. He can be trusted to see it through to completion and all of Scripture testifies to this truth.

God is not flawed like we are. As He says through the prophet Balaam, "God is not a man that he should lie, or a son of man that he should change his mind" (Numbers 23:19 ESV). Every word that God has spoken can be trusted because *He* can be trusted. The rainbow is our reminder of this. A perpetual symbol of the riches of His grace and the infallibility of His Word, it testifies of God's faithfulness to uphold His covenant. May we see it and remember—just as He does.

Where do you need to remember that God can be trusted? Take a moment to be still and invite the Holy Spirit to give you a verse—a promise—to hold on to. Place it somewhere you can regularly be reminded of it, and each time you read it, thank God that He is a promise-keeping God.

DAY ELEVEN

Shaped by History

PAULA MORRISON

Genesis 10

History was one of my favourite subjects at school—and growing up in the UK, there was a lot of it! In studying history, I found some of the answers to the questions I had as a child growing up in a divided nation; it explained how nations are formed, what causes other nations to be their enemy, and how that influences them going forward. These historical facts shaped my understanding of the world and my place in it; as Dr. Martin Luther King Jr. said: "We are not makers of history, we are made by history."

Genesis 10 reminds us that God is the maker of all history. Though it might be tempting to skip over these lists of names, they are our origins, the start of Israel's family tree and the birth of nations we know today. They tell a story, providing geographical reference points that were important to the original audience. In recording it, Moses provided the Israelites with a compact version of their history that could be easily memorized and shared down the generations; still today, the names are helpful in tracing the origins of all nations. Yet it isn't intended to be a complete historical record. Rather, it is a selective account that establishes the foundational lineages that lead to Abraham, to David, and ultimately, to Christ: the son of David, the son of Abraham, and the son of Adam.

On a more detailed level, this table lists the generations of Noah, starting from his three sons, who found the diverse ethnic groupings which spread over the earth post-Flood. The lines of Japheth and Shem are linked by Noah's blessing in Genesis 9:26-27. Noah asks God to extend Japheth's territory and for him to live in the tents of Shem, indicating for Shem to treat his younger brother with honour and his offspring as family.

In time, the sons of Japheth settled across modern Europe from Spain to Russia, while the sons of Shem occupied the Arabian Peninsula in the modern Middle East. It is from the nation formed from Shem's line that Abraham will come (Genesis 11:10-26) and how the Jewish nation will trace its heritage all the way to Jesus. Their history has become our history: This is the same geographical area where the Gospel went first to the Jew and then to the Gentile in the book of Acts. We as Gentile believers are grafted into this line of promise, descendants of Japheth welcomed in by Shem's descendants (Galatians 3:29).

By contrast, the sons of Ham became major enemies of the nation of Israel. Canaan in particular is connected with evil and opposition to God throughout Scripture, as are Egypt and Cush. This branch of Noah's family settled across West Africa and parts of Arabia were they lived as enemies of God and pursued evil practices (Deuteronomy 20:17-18). The curse on Canaan to be the lowest of slaves to his brothers is fulfilled when Joshua leads Israel into the Promised Land and Canaan becomes a servant to the children of Israel. Yet even these enemy peoples find their healing and redemption in Jesus (Matthew 15:21-28; John 4:4-26).

Finally, we must note the construction of the genealogy in addition to its contents. This table lists seventy names, representing the product of seven and ten, both numbers signifying completion and perfection to the ancient Hebrew mind. This is no coincidence. It is our perfect God who is the origin of our history, stretching back from the very beginning of nations forward to the culmination of the generations awaiting the Messiah at the coming of Jesus Christ. For us today, these verses point to God's faithfulness to all nations through the Gospel. We know this is true as we see the righteous line of Christ continue century after century, generation after generation, throughout all the world (Psalm 119:90).

Meditate on Psalm 119:90. As you reflect on God's faithfulness to the earliest generations, how can You see Him at work in your own family line? Give thanks for what He has been shaping throughout the past generations and commit those yet to come to His loving care.

The Path to Glory
NICOLE O'MEARA

Genesis 11:1-9

I used to sell make-up—the dumbest decision of my life.

After graduating college, I was excited for the job I was sure to find, a place to display my new knowledge. Instead, I found my life unchanged except for the addition of a lot of free time. I was sure God wanted me to use my intellect to succeed in life, so when those opportunities didn't come, I felt confused. In a hurry to find a way out of my discomfort, I joined a makeup sales team—despite the fact I couldn't sell water in a drought. Without consulting God, I chose a path I thought would bring me success. At a time when I should have been concentrating on where God was leading me, my focus drifted. I wasted time, energy, and money on an endeavour I didn't prayerfully consider.

God had called me to glorify Him first. Psalm 115:1 helped: "Not to us, O LORD, not to us, but to your name give glory." I could have picked a dozen different paths within His will, but I chose one that meandered outside it. He called me to glorify Him, but I chose a path that glorified myself.

In Genesis 11, we see a united people also intentionally choosing to glorify themselves. This is no meandering path; it is an expressway headed directly away from God. In Genesis 1:28 (and 9:1) God says, "Be fruitful and multiply and fill the earth.'" This is God's clear command for humanity. But in Babylon, the people throw off God's instructions and decide they know better. They desire to settle down and build an empire, reaching for the pre-eminence that belongs to God alone. In direct disobedience to God's command, they stay put and create idols out of their own wisdom.

Rebellion is not unique to the Babylonians, however. It has been man's default position from the moment Adam and Eve ate the forbidden fruit in hopes of becoming like God (Genesis 3:4-7). And we've all got a bit of Jonah in us, moving away from God when His command feels uncomfortable (Jonah 1:3). When we rebel, God has the power to bring us to a full stop, disciplining us with mercy and grace, giving us a chance to change our path.

In Babylon, "the LORD came down" (v.5), intervening and confusing the language of the people and scattering them to various locations. Their plan to stay put and glorify themselves is outright disobedience deserving of swift judgment. Righteous God could wipe them from the earth, but instead He graciously blocks their sinful path and mercifully disperses them. His intervention redirects the Babylonians, giving them an opportunity to reflect, repent, and return to His will.

Like the Babylonians, God moved me to a new town, providing a pocket of time to reflect on my choice to sell makeup and to change my path. Like Jonah in the belly of the great fish, our rebellion is often easier to spot when we are removed from the distractions of everyday life. And like Adam and Eve, when we step back onto the narrow path that leads to the heart of God, He lovingly forgives and welcomes us to walk beside him again.

Returning to right relationship with God is only possible because of Jesus. He paid the price for our rebellion, the ultimate act of grace, making a way for us to be near to a Holy God. God's redirections are meant to draw us back to the path He chose for us, for His glory and our good. Our willingness to be redirected is evidence of a growing faith, another gift of grace to our rebellious hearts.

Is there anywhere in your life that you have stepped off the path God has for you? Take a moment to repent, then invite the Lord to intervene and redirect your steps—for your good and His glory.

Familiar Places

ELLIE DI JULIO

Genesis 11:10-12:9

Every year around Christmas, I make the pilgrimage to my hometown to see my family and take a trip down memory lane. I drive by the house I was born in, pop into favourite shops, and revisit old memories. It's nostalgiatastic.

But there's more to these trips than re-experiencing my past. As I've matured, I've started to see my life's foundations with clearer eyes, understanding more of myself each time I visit by communing with this special place over and over.

God does this, as well, taking us back to familiar places as His own story matures and grows throughout the course of Scripture.

In particular, Genesis 12:6-7 introduces us to one of the Bible's most important, yet seemingly innocuous locations. Tired from a long journey, we find Abram making a pit stop after finally reaching Canaan. God is speaking to him again, promising that *this* is the land his descendants will inherit. And as powerful as that statement is, is where Abram stands when he hears it.

This location, just outside of Shechem, is mentioned constantly across both the Old and New Testaments as the site of pivotal moments in God's story.

It's the first place God appears to Abram in the Promised Land (Genesis 12:6-7). The land Jacob buys after reconciling with Esau (Genesis 18-20). The field where Joseph is betrayed (Genesis 37:12–14) and buried (Joshua 24:32). Where Moses instructs God's Law, blessings, and cursings to be kept (Deuteronomy 11:26-30; 27:1–8). Where Joshua dedicates the witness stone (Joshua 24:25). Where Israel is divided (1 Kings 12:16–17). Where Jesus reveals Himself as the Messiah to a Samaritan woman (John 4:4-26; 39-42).

But God isn't satisfied to bring us to a general location over and over; He tightens His focus to a single nearby tree.

We're told that "Abram passed through the land to the place of Shechem, as far as the terebinth tree of Moreh" (Genesis 12:6 NKJV). Now, terebinth trees are still fairly common in that region, but nothing in the Bible is without intention—this is more than a simple arboreal detail.

The terebinth is next mentioned some thousand years later as Isaiah receives his commission from God. He's told to prophesy Jerusalem's destruction yet is left with a hopeful note: "But as the terebinth and oak leave stumps when they are cut down, so the holy seed will be the stump in the land'" (Isaiah 6:13). This imagery is borne out by science; the terebinth's roots are so deep that it produces shoots even after being chopped down.

Sound familiar?

Later, as Isaiah begins to speak of the coming Messiah, he declares, "A shoot will come up from the stump of Jesse; from his roots a Branch will bear fruit" (Isaiah 11:1). This repetition instantly links us back to Isaiah 6:13, then as we look closer, back to the terebinth's tenacity, to Abram, to God's fulfilled promises, *and also forward* to the One who will come from the line of David, son of Jesse: Jesus (Matthew 1:1-17).

From unkillable tree to glorious life in Christ, God revisits this easily-overlooked location with us, each time adding to our understanding of His faithfulness, trustworthiness, and attention to our lives, down to the smallest detail.

As the years pass, and like a yearly pilgrimage home, we find ourselves circling back to places, people, and patterns we thought didn't matter but actually hold great significance, we can take comfort in knowing that the Master of detail is at work, folding it all together for the good of those who love Him (Romans 8:28).

Is there a 'place' in your story that God is inviting you to revisit? What new perspective does He want to give you there?

DAY FOURTEEN

Not by Sight

EMILY TYLER

Genesis 12:10-13:18

Ever had to share a piece of cake with a sibling? One person gets to cut and the other can choose their slice. I've watched my own children painstakingly observe, compare, and examine the pieces to ensure they give the best bit to the other. I'm kidding—of course they choose the piece that appears biggest and best for themselves!

When needing to divide the land due to its inability to feed and provide pasture for both Abram and Lot's flocks, Lot does much the same as my children when he looks around and sees the lush, well-watered plain of the Jordan. He prioritises possessions over people and "chose for himself" (Genesis 13:11) based on what he sees. He picks the biggest slice.

The problem with choosing for yourself based on sight is that you don't always get it right. Your slice of cake might be bigger, but it may have less frosting. Lot's choice to position himself near Sodom is problematic for a number of reasons:

He travels east. When Adam and Eve were kicked out of the Garden, they were sent eastwards. Throughout Genesis, moving east equals bad news.

He chooses the whole plain of Jordan. 'Jordan' means 'descender;' it's like death. What appears to be life-giving on the outside leads quickly down to the Dead Sea, waters in such an arid climate and so salty that nothing can live there.

His proximity to Sodom sucks him into sin. The next time we hear of Lot, he's no longer living near Sodom—he's living *in* Sodom (Genesis 14:12).

Lot doesn't think beyond instant gratification. Unlike Lot, Abram chooses the way of faith by trusting God's choice even when, in the short term, it appears to be the inferior one.

The loudest complaint when cake sharing goes wrong is, "It's not fair!" Human nature wants us to stand up for ourselves and fight for what's *rightfully* ours. As the patriarch of the family, it is Abram's right to pick first. It is his *right* to have the better piece of land. Yet, Abram chooses peace over possessions. He humbles himself and honours God by laying down his 'head of household' title, relinquishing his rights and preferring Lot. In doing so, he receives the seemingly smaller piece of cake.

But God has already promised that this land will be Abram's (Genesis 12:7). God waits for Lot to depart and then reminds Abram of this, directing him to "look around" because He is going to give it *all* to him and his offspring (Genesis 13:14-16). Not some, not a piece of the cake—all of it. Abram doesn't have to do anything; God says *He* will give it to him. Both Lot and Abram are looking at the same piece of land. Lot sees what is physically in front of him, but God calls Abram to see by faith what is coming.

We need God's perspective to see beyond the physical to the promise.

We are called to lay down our rights and live counter-culturally, "by faith, not sight" (2 Corinthians 5:7). We are called to choose God's way—people over possessions, peace over conflict, unseen over seen—and we do that by trusting God's Word.

Choosing land, or cake, can be a tricky business. But there's one choice we can make that will never fail us. This reward is bigger and better than we could dare to hope for (Ephesians 3:20), immediate *and* eternal. When we choose to believe in Jesus by faith, we are justified by His grace (Titus 3:7), and *God* becomes our portion. No inheritance or cake can ever beat that!

Where in your life do you feel like you've been left with the inferior portion? Take some time to lift up your eyes and 'look around.' What is the Holy Spirit showing you?

Kings and Priests

SINA STEELE

Genesis 14

I well remember my university days, eager to make new friends and enjoy my young adult years. I was headed on a downward trajectory of partying and living for myself—until Jesus appeared on the scene. *Sometimes, when we least expect it, when we're going about our everyday lives...suddenly, we encounter the Lord's presence, and everything changes.*

Kind of like the figure of Melchizedek. Seeming to appear out of nowhere, with no genealogy or lineage to place him in context, Melchizedek is an intriguing and mysterious character. The mention of him is brief, yet significant—almost like a cameo appearance in a film.

Abram is returning from war when he encounters Melchizedek in Genesis 14. All we're told is that "Melchizedek king of Salem brought out bread and wine. He was priest of God Most High, and he blessed Abram, saying, 'Blessed be Abram by God Most High, Creator of heaven and earth. And praise be to God Most High, who delivered your enemies into your hand.'" (vv.18-20). How few these words are, yet what significance they carry.

Melchizedek is an enigmatic figure who has stumped many scholars. He is a king, yet also a priest, who somehow knows and serves Yahweh. Pre-dating the establishment of the Levitical priesthood, he blesses Abram right there and then in the city of Salem (which means 'peace') and even brings out bread and wine for him (foreshadowing communion). Salem would later become known as Jerusalem, the centre of the land promised to Abraham, as well as the central city of the Biblical narrative.

Aside from this encounter, there are only two other references to Melchizedek in Scripture: once in Psalm 110 and again in Hebrews. While these passages don't provide any additional background information for us, they do make it clear that Melchizedek is a type of Christ, a foreshadowing of our Royal Priest, and that, unlike the Levitical priesthood, who continually needed to offer sacrifices for their sins and the sins of others, Jesus' priesthood is perfect. He is declared "a priest forever, in the order of Melchizedek" (Hebrews 7:17), who, with one single sacrifice, has made atonement for all (v.27).

When Abram meets Melchizedek, his response is to give him a tenth of all he has acquired out on the battlefield—*before* tithing is ever instituted in the Bible (Genesis 14:20). *How could Abram know to tithe when a law has never been given?* Abram seems to instinctively recognise the office of the person standing before him and seeks to appropriately honour Melchizedek. So should our response be when Jesus appears on the scene, our great High Priest and mediator of the New Covenant, the One who gave it all for us, the One to whom we owe everything.

I encountered Jesus during my university years, at a time when I was not searching for Him. In fact, I was actively moving in an opposite direction, focused on living for myself. But when He appeared, life suddenly changed. I didn't understand it all, have perfect theology, or know the 'right' Christian lingo—I just knew I had encountered someone whose presence changed my heart. And just like Abram tithed to Melchizedek, without any law telling him to, so did I want to offer my all to Jesus—because it's to Him it rightly belongs.

Melchizedek's name means 'king of righteousness,' and what a perfect way to describe Jesus; He is the true King of Righteousness, our Prince of Peace. When He appears in our story, it may seem like a mystery or an enigma, yet His presence changes everything. He pronounces a blessing over us and a feast of 'bread and wine'—His own body and blood sacrificed for us (Luke 22:17-20)—and our heart response can be nothing less than giving back to Him what is already rightfully His: our time, our relationships, our talents, our conversations, our strengths, our finances—our *everything*.

Is there anything you have been withholding from God? What might it look like for you to offer Him this part of your life as an act of worship?

Our Very Great Reward

AIMEE WALKER

Genesis 15

I was a young girl when I first read Genesis 15:1: "Do not be afraid, Abram. I am your shield, your very great reward." I was so in awe of the idea that I wrote it down in a little notebook. The idea stayed with me, but as I grew older, I also grew jaded, and sometimes this promise didn't seem quite enough. I wanted answers to my specific problems—to my longed-for breakthroughs—more than I wanted Him.

Abram wrestles with this, too.

He's just returned from a war in which he not only recovered his nephew, Lot, who had been kidnapped by enemy kings (Genesis 14:12), but also acquired a great many spoils—riches that originally belonged to the King of Sodom but were now rightfully his. Abram tithed of those spoils to the mysterious King Melchizedek (v.20), but he also did something else: He swore an oath to God that he would not keep anything, not even a thread or the strap of a sandal, lest the King of Sodom take credit for making Abram rich (vv.22-23). Credit that Abram knew belonged to God alone. It is in the context of this faith-filled act that God appears to Abram, revealing Himself as his shield and true reward.

What a promise—the gift, the reward, of God Himself! And yet, Abram's response to this message is tinged by disappointment, perhaps even cynicism. While God has greatly prospered him, he is still waiting for the descendants and the land God previously promised, and so he says, "Sovereign Lord, what can you give me since I remain childless and the one who will inherit my estate is Eliezer of Damascus?" (Genesis 15:2). Abram doesn't want a servant to inherit his possessions and position. He wants a son, a child of his own body who will bear his name and likeness, who will carry on the promise.

And God's father heart has the same cry. He doesn't want slaves but sons and daughters. He wants to build a family to inherit all that He has promised and prepared for them.

In response to Abram's questions, God takes him outside and shows him the stars, telling him that if he can count them all he can count how numerous his offspring will one day be. He also assures him that his descendants will one day possess the land He has said they will. Abram believes God's promise of a son, but of the land he asks, "How can I be sure?" (v.8).

So with a covenantal sacrifice, God seals his promises to Abram. He has Abram prepare the sacrificial animals, and as night falls and Abram sleeps, the symbols of God's presence pass between the divided animals (v.17). Usually, both parties to the covenant would walk through them, but that night, only God does, taking full responsibility for the execution of this covenant. Like the Noahic Covenant, this, too, is a covenant of grace. All God requires of Abram is that by faith he receives what God has done on his behalf.

It's all He asks of us, as well, because the Cross, too, is a covenant of grace. On that day, Jesus took full responsibility for our sins—for the cost of the old covenant being broken—and gave us the right through faith to become children of God. When we choose to receive what Jesus has done, we are no longer slaves to sin trying to earn our place, but sons and daughters destined to inherit what God has promised.

When life seems to oppose this truth and we find ourselves wrestling with disappointment, just like He did for Abram, God comes alongside us and demonstrates His grace in the midst of our weakness, declaring: "Don't be afraid. I am your shield and your very great reward."

Where do you need to allow God to be your reward in this season? As you process where He is inviting you to trust Him to be enough for you, don't be afraid to ask questions and voice your disappointments—your Father wants to hear His child's heart. Listen carefully for His response.

A Series of Firsts

ASHLEY KELLEY

Genesis 16

Do you ever get annoyed by the seemingly insignificant side stories included in movies and books? I prefer to stay with the action, to follow the main story. Over the years, however, I have learned that character development is an important part of storytelling, and side stories are used to give the audience glimpses into different aspects of the characters.

In the story of Genesis, we could easily read the portions of Scripture about Hagar and Ishmael as superfluous because, after all, they aren't part of the new family God is establishing through Abram. Here's the truth, however: Their side story is vital to our understanding of the whole. Through it we have the opportunity to learn more about the narrative's main character—not Hagar or Ishmael but God Himself.

The journey out into the wilderness with Hagar is worth the effort of trudging through the sand and sweating in the heat of the day. As we sit alongside her near the refreshing spring, watching what happens when the Angel of the Lord greets her, we find ourselves in awe of who our God is revealed to be. There are a few firsts that happen in this encounter between Hagar and the Angel of the Lord, and we learn something about God through each one of them.

First up: the Angel of the Lord. The first time this being appears to anyone in the Bible is right here with Hagar (Genesis 16:7). There are differing theories concerning *who* the Angel of the Lord is—an early appearance of Christ, a physical appearance of the Father, or, at the very least, a representative of God, acting in His full authority. Whichever theory we prefer, the reality is that he reveals God's actions and words. In this appearance, the Angel of the Lord shows us that God comes near to us in our despair. He is a very real depiction of the often-quoted Psalm 34:18: "The Lord is close to the brokenhearted and saves those who are crushed in spirit."

In the next first, God, through the Angel of the Lord, names someone before their birth. We have no record of this happening until this moment with Hagar in the wilderness. In her deepest struggle, God eases her pain by acknowledging her situation and using it as an opportunity to reveal more of Himself to her. "You shall name him Ishmael," is the directive given to her (v.11), a name which literally means 'God hears.' This is to remind Hagar that He has heard her misery; He is aware of her pain. Every time the baby will cry, every time Hagar will comfort him, every time she will say his name—she will be reminded that God Almighty hears her. She will remember how God revealed Himself and comforted her in her despair.

Finally, for the first time, someone gives a name to God. It is clearly written that Hagar calls Him *El Roi*, "the God who sees me" (v.13). She has learned first-hand that God—the One so big and powerful He stands outside time—isn't too big to notice her. He is a God who sees, a God who hears, and a God who comes near.

Hagar's wilderness journey, a side story that could easily be breezed through in the larger narrative of Genesis, reveals to us precious insight into the character and heart of our God. In our deepest struggles and darkest times, we have a God who deeply, intimately cares about each of us, just as He did for Hagar.

What names of God are meaningful to you in this season and why? Take some time to thank Him for how He has already revealed Himself to you, and ask if there are new names that He wants you to know Him by.

Guilty by Assumption
ASHLEY KELLY

Genesis 17

I'm not much of a re-reader. I can count on one hand how many books I have read more than once (the Bible not included). Something happens when we revisit a story: We come to the text with the end in mind, knowing how it all comes together. As the reader, we know the characters' mistakes and where their decisions will take them. Because of that, we tend to impose our knowledge onto the characters, forgetting their limited perspective.

The temptation to do just that exists even when we read the Bible. I have been guilty of imposing my knowledge of Abraham's completed life onto the beginning and middle as he is living it. *How many times have I heard this story? How many times have I read about Hagar and Ishmael, knowing this isn't the son through whom God intends to fulfil His promise of countless descendants?* Yet every time, I assume that Abraham knows it, too.

By the time we arrive at Genesis 17, it has been thirteen years since we last saw or heard anything about Abram—now Abraham. Thirteen years since Hagar bore him a son. Thirteen years since there has been any record of God speaking directly to him. I wonder: *For thirteen years, has Abraham lived fulfilled as a father because of Ishmael? Has he assumed Ishmael is the one through whom his offspring will become as numerous as the stars (Genesis 15:5)?*

If we approach the text by first setting aside what we know already and our modern cultural biases, we see the story in a whole new light. Abraham is the patriarch of a new family God is creating. He comes from a lineage and cultural background that was not founded upon God's Law, for that has not yet been given nor will it be for hundreds of years. Barrenness was shameful and a common cause for divorce in the ancient world because of the importance of continuing the family line. Sarai—now Sarah—cannot carry out her responsibility as a wife. Understanding this, it isn't shocking for Abraham and Sarah to turn to Hagar to birth an heir for Abraham and to view Ishmael as the solution to their problem.

Interestingly, Sarah is not even mentioned in the previous promises God made to Abraham (Genesis 12:2, 15:5). It isn't until nearly twenty-five years later that God reveals she is part of them. In fact, God finally gives the promise a name, and it isn't Ishmael: "'Sarah will bear you a son, and you will call him Isaac. I will establish my covenant with him as an everlasting covenant for his descendants after him'" (v.19). As a father, this must be a difficult thing to hear—that the son he already has, already loves, is not the promised one. Abraham and Sarah now have to come to terms with what this reiterated and clarified promise now means: There will be another son. Their way of fulfilling the promise was, in fact, not God's way.

We're often guilty of the same thinking, of making the same assumptions about God's plan. It's tempting to assume our own desires and ideas are what He must have for us. We may even find ourselves in situations similar to Abraham and Sarah—attempting to fulfil God's promises in our own way and time. The truth is, however, that we don't get to determine how God brings about His promises. That job belongs to Him alone. He is the Author and Finisher of not only our faith but also this whole grand story He is weaving together (Hebrews 12:2). Our job is to follow Him faithfully, refraining from trying to jump ahead or imposing our own ideas upon Him. It is His story, after all. May we recognize the amazing privilege of simply being invited into it.

Spend some time sitting with your own story. How has assumption or running ahead of God gotten you into trouble? How have you seen Him redeem your story in spite of this?

Looking for Hope

JENNA MARIE MASTERS

Genesis 18:1-15

A mama bird once decided to build her nest in our rotting patio cover. She was the best mama, tirelessly tending to life among the decay. I had hoped we would tear down the cover and replace it with beautiful wood but now found myself praying it would stay up a while longer. I was rooting for the hope of new life.

We're often eager to bulldoze the things that aren't perfectly lovely in our life; we don't want to have to squint to see the potential. The world doesn't have patience for this. It preaches that if your marriage is struggling, end it. If your friend betrays you, cut them off. If your body grows weary of persisting, stop trying.

This is the world's way. It is not God's way.

Don't bring in the demolition crew so quickly. Instead, look for hope, even if the promise is huddled in a fragile shell.

That is what God does when He looks at us. What Sarah sees as "worn out" and "too old," God sees as a vessel for His glory (Genesis 18:12). In the barren woman, He catches a glimpse of faith. And where there is faith, miracles are born. Because "by faith even Sarah, who was past childbearing age, was enabled to bear children because she considered him faithful" (Hebrews 11:11). Yes, Sarah laughs when God says He will fulfil His promise through her old bones, but she does not laugh at the Promiser. Because even "if we are faithless, He remains faithful" (2 Timothy 2:13).

God allowed a baby to be born from faith's seed. Seeds are small. Sometimes our faith will be almost imperceptible—cling to hope anyway. When you're holding broken bits of a marriage, friendship, career, finances, or health in your hands, think of Sarah. Offer up the pieces, along with all the faith you can muster, and trust that God can do a mighty work. Think of the delicate egg perched in our dilapidated patio, holding the possibility of life and death, and of the mama bird focused on signs of life, just like our God looks for signs of faith. *Why would rickety boards or an old lady's bones discourage Him?!* Just as He says to Abraham and Sarah: "Is anything too hard for the Lord?" (Genesis 18:14).

Jesus wants us to look at the mountain in front of us, and in faith, tell it to move (Matthew 17:20).

Even when we feel faithless, we can follow the example of the disciples and ask God to increase our faith (Luke 17:5). When we're brave enough to do this, we're acknowledging that God's ways are not our ways (Isaiah 55:8–9). Birthing new life from old bones is God's way; letting a baby bird hatch in a termite palace is God's way. Patiently hover over these truths. Ask for the Holy Spirit to breathe life into every situation. Try not to focus on the broken boards framing the circumstances but surrender to the craftsman of your soul.

What have you been tempted to 'bulldoze' in your own life? Grab a blank piece of paper and brainstorm with the Holy Spirit. What 'seeds of hope' is God inviting you to see? How can you partner with Him and plant those seeds?

 Drawing Near

SHELLEY JOHNSON

Genesis 18:16-33

I have a tendency to worry about my children. When I discovered that other mums felt the same, a few of us banded together to turn our worries into prayers. Every week for over a decade, we gathered to pour out all our hopes and concerns for our children to our Father in Heaven. We spoke God's promises over them and, over the years, learned how to trust God with the outcomes. Those Friday mornings were special, set apart days because we intentionally drew near to God to intercede for those most precious to us.

Similarly driven by worry, Abraham intercedes for the righteous in the wicked cities of Sodom and Gomorrah in Genesis 18. Nowhere else in Scripture do we see Abraham so passionately pray for anyone, not even his family. Faced with the thought of any righteous person dying at the hand of God, Abraham steps into the role of a bold supplicant, becoming our first model for the way of the intercessor.

When we read that "Abraham approached [God]" (v.23), in the truest sense of the original language, Abraham is stepping into closer physical proximity with His Father to make the desires of his heart known. He draws near to pray.

God opens this door for Abraham when He invites him into conversation about His coming judgment on the evil cities. God looks upon this man with whom He has an intimate, covenantal relationship and chooses to share His plans; Abraham accepts the invitation and steps forward with reverence, remembering his lowly place as mere dust and God's sovereign role as Judge of all the earth. He draws near to God with both holy fear and humble boldness to speak his heart on behalf of others.

When we look at this divine discussion between the Creator and the created, we recognize that God remains fully engaged with Abraham. He doesn't argue. He never yells. Instead, He listens to Abraham with grace and kindness, relenting at every ask. As Matthew Henry puts it, God "did not leave off granting till Abraham left off asking." Not because Abraham is a superhuman prayer warrior but because they share a deeply-rooted relationship. God can see that Abraham's motivation derives from a source of love and concern for the righteous. Likewise, Abraham trusts God's goodness and wisdom. Back and forth the dialogue proceeds with Abraham's bold requests and God's willing responses, revealing the intimacy between them.

This is intercession.

The moment we choose to follow Jesus Christ, the Holy Spirit fills us, and we become covenantal people like Abraham. As such, we, too, are invited into dialogue with the Father. When our hearts are moved for someone, we can confidently enter into His presence and call on Him for action, crying out on their behalf. The way God answers Abraham's appeals gives us solid evidence that not only are our prayers heard, but that they matter. God's willingness to save an entire evil city for the sake of ten righteous people demonstrates His heart for Abraham—so much so that even when no righteous can be found, God makes sure to save Abraham's family (Genesis 19:15).

Each time we draw near to God with hearts full of love and concern, we can think of Abraham's intercessory prayers for Sodom and Gomorrah, remembering how Abraham steps away from these prayers full of faith, trusting God with the outcome. We, too, can pray with such faith because Abraham has shown us that our prayers are received by a God who welcomes our presence and petitions. We can trust that our Father hears our prayers and responds to them in the most perfect, just, and holy ways.

Who or what is God inviting you to draw near and intercede for? Spend some time in focused prayer being careful not only to ask, but also to listen. Record anything that you sense God speaking to you and keep prayerfully contending for what He has revealed.

Small Sins, Big Deal

TRISTANY CORGAN

Genesis 19:1-29

I struggle with a lot of 'small sins.' Things like holding a grudge, gossiping about a coworker, complaining about my circumstances, or telling a little white lie. These actions seem so small that I often sweep them under the rug and act as if they don't matter. After all, I'm not killing anyone or stealing someone's car. However, our small sins often morph into bigger sins, and our big sins often morph into egregious ones.

This is what we see happening in Sodom and Gomorrah.

The people of Sodom probably committed relatively 'small' sins at first. Maybe they began by entertaining lustful fantasies about others. Perhaps they then acted out those fantasies and began sleeping with anyone they desired. By the time we reach Genesis 19, they have descended into acts that have become more and more wicked until it is now normal for the men in town to desire to rape the two angels who have come from Abraham's house (Genesis 18:16, 19:5). Their sins have become so great that God has decided to destroy the city and everyone in it, echoing the judgment of the Flood (Genesis 6:7).

The idea that God would eradicate an entire city may seem harsh or even wrong to us. But we must remember two things: Every person in Sodom is guilty of sin and deserving of punishment; there are not even ten righteous people living there (Genesis 18:32). And because God is holy, righteous, and just, He cannot allow sin to go unpunished; to do so would go against His character. He always does what is good and right.

Yet God's wrath and justice are not His only qualities we observe here. God is also rich in mercy for His people, and He shows mercy to the only righteous man in town, Lot, and his family by providing a way for them to escape the judgment of Sodom and leading them safely out by the hand (Genesis 19:16).

God does the same thing for us. Because of the sin nature we inherit from Adam and Eve, we deserve punishment and death. But God has mercifully provided an escape through the death and resurrection of His Son, Jesus (Romans 5:8-9).

However, while we are indeed saved and justified at the moment we put our faith in Jesus, we face temptation for sins both big and small for the rest of our lives. Lot and his family surely do, even after they leave Sodom (Genesis 19:26 & 31-32). Immediately following their narrow escape, Lot's wife looks back and becomes a pillar of salt. The Hebrew word used for her action, *nabat*, refers to regarding something with favour or pleasure. Lot's wife isn't just glancing over her shoulder at the destruction; she is gazing upon her old life with favour. But her old life was unrighteous, and our righteous God cannot allow unrighteousness to go unpunished. So she is swept away with the rest of the city.

Though we cannot be condemned once we've been justified by Jesus (Romans 8:1), we must learn from Lot's wife's mistake and be careful not to look upon our old, sinful ways with fondness. The 'small sins' we commit in secret may not seem like that big of a deal, but they *are* a big deal to our just and righteous God. Yet He is also gracious and faithful, and He has mercifully offered us an escape from temptation (1 Corinthians 10:13). Instead of gazing upon our old ways with favour, we must fix our gaze upon Jesus, the Author and Finisher of our faith who has defeated both sin and death (Hebrews 12:2; 1 Peter 2:24). It is only when we fix our eyes on Him that we are forgiven and freed.

Is there anything that the Holy Spirit has been bringing conviction about that you have been dismissing as 'no big deal'? Spend some time asking Him what the way forward looks like in that area, then commit to stop looking back and thank Jesus that He enables you to step freely onto the new path He has shown you.

A Way of Escape
CARA RAY

Genesis 19:30-38

Lot's nerves are raw. It is as though he is living in a bad dream. Only this isn't a dream, it is reality. Within a few days, he has lost everything he owned and most of his family. He knows he should be relieved that he is alive, but all he feels is shock and grief.

Now far from the smoldering ash of what used to be Sodom, Lot's troubles are still not over. While his presence in Zoar has spared it from also being destroyed, Lot is afraid to stay. His fear drives him to flee into the mountains and settle in a cave.

Away from the masses of people and the pervasive wickedness of Sodom and Gomorrah, Lot may be assuming he is on the downhill side of his trials. Unfortunately, not only does destruction lie behind Lot, but because he is unprepared for temptation, it also lies in front of him. His daughters are fearful of their lack of prospects and of an unknown future, so they devise a wicked plan at their father's expense.

There's little doubt the depravity and sexual perversion they had grown accustomed to in Sodom influence their thinking and actions. They have no regard for the sanctity of sex within marriage, and they saw how casually their father had offered them to the sex-crazed mob at the door of their house (Genesis 19:8). To them, sex is anything but holy; it is a bargaining chip, a tool, a weapon of control.

Their twisted plan is to get their father drunk and sleep with him so they can bear children by him. Successful in their mission, they bear two sons, named Moab and Ammon. From these two sons come forth two enemy nations of Israel: the Moabites and Ammonites. They are referred to with contempt throughout Scripture as "the children of Lot" (Psalm 83:5-8; Deuteronomy 2:9 &19 KJV).

Lot's daughters bear the weight of their depravity and sinful actions, but Lot is not without blame. Lot seeks to escape his painful reality by numbing himself with alcohol. With his guard down, he relinquishes control and sin runs rampant, bearing painful consequences in his life.

We can attempt to escape reality with lots of different vices. During a painful period in my life, I tried to escape my grief, not with alcohol, but with busyness. I thought if I could distract myself with something productive, I wouldn't have to deal with the grief I felt. Even 'good' things can become 'bad' or 'distracting' when we use them to numb ourselves or pull away from our problems. Lot's life reminds us that a temporary escape only increases or prolongs our troubles.

First Corinthians 10:13 offers us hope and a strategy for when temptation to sin strikes: "No temptation has overtaken you except what is common to mankind. And God is faithful; he will not let you be tempted beyond what you can bear. But when you are tempted, he will also provide a way out so that you can endure it." Whatever temptations we face, they won't shock God; He is faithful and will provide a way of escape. It doesn't always have a blinking neon exit sign, but there is a path of obedience in every sticky situation and a way to refuse to submit to whatever temporarily satisfies but isn't Christ.

No matter where Lot lived, he couldn't escape sin, and neither can we; it's everywhere because it's within every human heart (Jeremiah 17:9). Our refuge isn't found in escaping our problems but in the person of Jesus Christ. Run to him the next time temptation strikes. The satisfaction that He offers is better than any temporary relief we might find somewhere else. He is our way of escape, no matter what lies behind or before us.

What are you trying to escape in this season? What might it look like practically for you to find your refuge in Jesus? What changes might you need to make for this to be possible?

Embracing Reverent Awe

ADÉLE DEYSEL

Genesis 20

The first decade of my Christian walk was dominated by a fear of God's judgement. I was *that* person, raising my hand at every altar call. When it came to counting salvations each Sunday, I was a sure thing—they could 'count me in' the moment I walked through the door. With the stories of God's wrath echoing in my mind, I would sit and analyse every choice I had made that week. Filled with fear, shame, and condemnation, I was left wondering if something was wrong with me. Everyone else appeared to have their life together, but walking the 'straight and narrow' seemed impossible to me.

If God is so loving, *why was I so afraid?* I needed to understand what it actually means to fear the Lord.

Most of the words used in Scripture to describe fear carry a dual meaning: They can mean both 'to be afraid or terrified' *and* 'to reverence.' We see these different responses play out in Genesis 20.

Here, Abraham has been up to his old tricks—lying to kings by saying his wife is only his sister. Consequently, Sarah has been taken into Abimelek's harem. God warns Abimelek in a dream that he will die if Sarah is not returned to her husband. When he informs his officials of this, they are understandably afraid (v.8). In their day, a punitive deity causing ruthless fear amongst their subjects was the commonly-held belief; a God of love and grace was unheard of. And so the word to describe their fear, *yārē*, here conveys the terror of their impending judgement.

Abimelek confronts Abraham about his deceit, and ironically, Abraham tries to justify his actions by saying, "I thought surely there is no fear of God in this place" (v. 11). But in this context, 'fear' (*yir'á*) means something different; it is describing moral, reverent awe and respect for God— something Abraham had no expectation of finding in Gerar.

Abimelek meets God in a dream and then acts out of a fear of condemnation, not conviction. For the unbeliever, fear of God means being afraid of His wrath and judgment. God is the author of morality and has the authority to execute judgement, and when we are not reconciled to Him through

Christ, we will live in fear of His holiness and righteousness revealed to us through His wrath.

My own fearful response was caused by being insecure in my salvation. I had a lack of biblical understanding, and the enemy used this to isolate me and hold me hostage; his accusations made me reluctant to freely approach God. Only fearing punishment leads to isolation and losing objectivity and perspective, which leads to faithless responses. If the enemy succeeds in making us scared of God, he removes our dependence on Him; instead of living in God's love, we end up living in fear.

Yes, I was afraid, but facing my fear of judgement guided me towards understanding the hope of my salvation through Christ. God takes our mistakes and turns them into a masterpiece for His glory, using sinful humans to accomplish His purposes.

When reading about God's wrath, let us press in deeper and seek His love and grace. It is true that His righteousness calls for His response through judgement, but our hope is found in His proven love for us. As Psalm 111:10 tells us, "Fear of the Lord is the foundation of true wisdom." Our heart posture towards God determines our perspective, and being grounded in the truth of His Word determines our response. Embracing a reverent awe of God—rather than terror—will lead to faithful responses, freedom from condemnation (Romans 8:1), and peace that surpasses all understanding (Philippians 4:6).

When we fear God, we can face anything.

How would you describe your own fear of God—are you afraid of Him or do you behold Him with reverent awe? Why is this? If you have a tendency to be afraid, invite the Holy Spirit to pour the love of the Father into your heart (Romans 5:5) that His perfect love might cast out your fear (1 John 4:18).

With Eyes Wide Open

AMBER PALMER

Genesis 21:1-21

Sometimes life throws us curve balls, taking us down roads we never wanted to go down. The answers to our prayers look different to what we hoped for, and in the wilderness of unmet expectation, disappointment weighs heavy. Feeling empty, alone, and helpless, we believe the lie that it's the end of our story. *But God.* When God enters the scene, His presence changes everything, and we realise that what felt like the end is only just the beginning.

In Genesis 21, we find Hagar back in a familiar place. Feeling afresh the sting of rejection, Abraham has banished her and her son Ishmael to the desert of Beersheba. With their water supplies gone, she is sobbing, brokenhearted at the thought of having to watch her child die. But God, full of mercy and grace, meets her in the midst of her pain. Just as He did before (Genesis 16:9-12), He lovingly opens Hagar's eyes, reminding her He hears and will be faithful to His promises for her and Ishmael.

As much as Hagar doesn't want to be in the wilderness, it is the place where she repeatedly encounters God. As an Egyptian servant, who more than likely grew up believing in multiple gods, the wilderness allows her to experience the one true God. Desperate situations often leave our hearts and eyes wide open to God. Sometimes it takes us being out in the middle of nowhere, alone, destitute, and poured out, in order to hear God and choose Him over everything else. It is in such times that God doesn't have to vie for our attention. At the end of ourselves, we finally draw nearer to Him, His voice becoming crystal clear against the silence of the empty land.

God doesn't take Hagar and Ishmael from the wilderness, though. Instead, He creates a life for them right where they are, enabling them to lean on Him in ways they wouldn't be able to if He simply removed them from their difficult circumstances. God sustains them, provides safety, and fulfils the promises He gave to them. In all the ways Hagar feels she is lacking, the wilderness provides an abundance to her from God. There, she becomes seen, heard, and connected to the One who hears her cries when no one else will.

Oftentimes we find ourselves in the wilderness because we become too distraught to make sense of our situation. Our soul becomes parched as we try to survive on our own. We forget about the hope there is in God, and we can become blinded from seeing the true Source we need. Hagar's outlook drastically changes when God opens her eyes to see the well of water. Where previously there was only death as an option, the well brings life to her and her son. Jesus is our well of water. Death was once our only option in the wilderness of sin, but Jesus cleanses us and brings eternal life. He gives us access to the source of living water—the Holy Spirit. Revelation 7:16-17 reminds us that "(t)hey shall hunger no more, neither thirst anymore; the sun shall not strike them, nor any scorching heat. For the Lamb in the midst of the throne will be their shepherd, and he will guide them to springs of living water, and God will wipe away every tear from their eyes." We will be saved from the wilderness of this earth by the living water forevermore because Jesus changes everything!

When we find ourselves in the wilderness, we must ask God to open our eyes to the life and hope there is in Jesus. With our eyes wide open, we will be able to drink deeply of His living water and experience the abundance of the Lord—even in desert places.

Wherever you are sitting as you read this, open your eyes and intentionally look around. What is God inviting you to see in your physical environment that you might have been overlooking? Now ask Him to do the same for you in the spiritual realm.

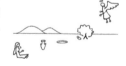

Gracious Assertiveness

CARA RAY

Genesis 21:22-34

Knowing how to conduct ourselves uprightly in business isn't always as black and white as we'd like it to be. When faced with an obstacle, *when do we act with generosity to benefit others, and when do we protect what is rightfully ours?*

For over a decade, my husband and I served on the board of directors of a school where all of our children attended. As board members, it was our primary duty to steward the organization as property of the Lord. However, we often felt the tension of making policies that were in the best interests of the school even when it wasn't what we wanted for our family. Knowing when to relinquish our rights and when to protect them required much wisdom and discernment.

It's comforting to know this isn't a modern dilemma; Abraham struggled with this balance, as well.

Abraham had the distinct privilege of knowing God was going to give him land, multiply his descendents, and make him a great blessing to the nations (Genesis 12:1-3). Yet when he could've enjoyed his divine privilege to the land, he graciously gave Lot the first choice of where to live, choosing to lay the groundwork for a healthy long-term relationship with his extended family (Genesis 13).

Here in Genesis 21, Abraham is once more at a crossroads of deciding how to dwell in peace with his neighbours. But instead of relinquishing his rights to his neighbour as he did with Lot, this time, he stands up for them. His household is growing rapidly in the land, and their ability to continue to flourish is dependent on having a reliable water source. The nearby well is rightfully his, but Abimelek's servants have been using it— and negotiating an agreement might prove to be difficult given the history between Abraham and this foreign king.

Some years earlier, when Abraham and Sarah were in the Philistine city of Gerar, Abimelek had taken notice of Sarah (Genesis 20). She was beautiful, and he wanted her for his harem. Abraham was afraid they would kill him, so he told a half-truth: that Sarah was his sister. Instead of taking a stand, Abraham fearfully took a seat, bringing tension and potential future conflict into his relationship with a neighbouring nation.

Despite their past run-in and this blight on Abraham's character, Abimelek cannot deny that the one true God is with Abraham, blessing him in all that he does (Genesis 21:22). The king wisely interprets the Lord's favour upon Abraham as a potential threat. He knows that, with God's blessing, Abraham's offspring might supplant his own kingdom in the future; thus, making peace with him now will be advantageous.

So Abimelek approaches Abraham to create a covenant between them. This time, though, Abraham doesn't skirt the issue and deals more honestly with Abimelek. He asserts his rights to the well and confronts Abimelek about his servant's use of his property. Yet, even in this confrontation, Abraham exhibits grace, sealing the covenant by giving Abimelek seven ewe lambs and naming the place *Beersheba*, meaning "the well of the oath" (v.31).

This ancient conflict over water rights might at first glance seem inconsequential to our modern lives, but there are lessons for us in the consequences Abraham previously bore due to his lack of assertiveness and the wisdom he embodies here when he extends grace. Abraham learned through his mistakes to assert himself and trust God to provide the right outcome. Even as he blunders through many of his business dealings, we see God's invisible hand of provision working to fulfil His promises to Abraham. We, too, will fail at striking the perfect balance of love for others and sticking up for our rights. Thankfully, God still graciously asserts His will in our lives, despite our many failures, and we can trust Him.

Where in your life do you struggle to be assertive? Invite the Holy Spirit to show you what it looks like practically to marry grace and boldness there.

Like Father, Like Son

AIMÉE WALKER

Genesis 22

My girls were born with glitter in their veins. When they were little, they loved to dress up as princesses and reenact their favourite fairy tales, but at times, the lines between fantasy and reality got a little blurred, and it was hard for them to discern fact from fiction. As we read the familiar Sunday School stories of Scripture, the lines can get somewhat blurred for us, too. We forget that these were real people—not fanciful stories but actual events.

A perfect example of this is found in Genesis 22, where we find the last two recorded conversations between God and Abraham. These final interactions have echoes of the first: an instruction to go somewhere that God will later show him and a promise of blessing. But this time, God asks something of Abraham that will cost him everything. He asks him to take his son, Isaac, and sacrifice him as a burnt offering (v.2). *Can you even imagine?*

We read these conversations with the end in mind, knowing that Isaac is spared when God provides a ram to be sacrificed in his place (v.13). From our stance in history, we see a beautiful foreshadowing of the sacrifice of Jesus that secured our freedom. But Abraham doesn't know any of this. He only knows what God has asked of him and what God has promised. And as he weighs these things, his response is to get up early the next morning and set out to do the unthinkable.

Every step that Abraham takes towards Moriah is a step of actively surrendered obedience—an act of worship.

But he isn't the only one taking those steps.

Genesis 21 closes with Isaac newly weaned, and because of this, many have assumed that he is still a child when Abraham is asked to sacrifice him. But the events of Genesis 22 occur "some time later" (v.1), and based on Sarah's age when she dies (Genesis 23:1-2), rabbinic tradition places him at the age of about 37. Isaac is not a child with no say in the matter; he is a full-grown man who trusts and co-operates with what his father is doing. Twice, Genesis 22 tells us that Abraham and Isaac walk *together*—once before Isaac knows that he is the sacrifice and once after (vv.6 & 8). This account is not just of Abraham's surrendered faith but also of Isaac's; together they point us to how the Father and Jesus walk in unity of purpose and to Christ's willingness to lay down His life (John 10:17-18).

Faith calls us to surrender our own will in order to make room in our lives for *His* will. We can only do this if we keep the truth of who God is firmly in view. This is what enables Abraham to walk in surrender through his most painful and costly trial yet. He knows God has said that it is through Isaac that his descendants will come, and he knows that God is faithful to what He promises—so he keeps looking up. As he walks, he lifts up his eyes (v.4) and sees the mountain God told him about; he has received guidance. He will later lift up his eyes (v.13) and see the ram, beholding God's provision.

Abraham's willingness to surrender leads both him and Isaac to experience God in a new way: as *Jehovah Jireh*, the One who provides. And God rewards his faithfulness, reaffirming His promise and extending it further with the declaration that "your seed [Jesus] shall possess the gate of His enemy. In your seed all the nations of the earth will be blessed—because you obeyed My voice" (Genesis 22:17-18 TLV).

Like Abraham and Isaac, we are called to walk with God in obedient surrender, lifting our eyes to see His faithful provision, and offering ourselves as living sacrifices. As Paul teaches, this is the "true and proper" response to God's mercy and the way of transformation (Romans 12:1-2).

Where is God inviting you to take a step of surrendered obedience? What do you need to remember about His character to be able to follow where He is leading you?

Sorrow's Pull

SHELLEY JOHNSON

Genesis 23

As I recently attended a friend's funeral, the irony of death did not escape me: The one who dies is made whole and given eternal life in Heaven, while those still on earth are left to feel death's grip and sorrows. For those of us who remain, when grief threatens to swallow us whole and keep us rooted in the soil of sadness, we find it difficult to rise up and move on.

This is where we find Abraham—at the bedside of his beloved wife, Sarah, who has died in the land of the Hittites. Though the words are few, we are given a glimpse of the depth of Abraham's sorrows as he kneels "to mourn for Sarah and to weep over her" (Genesis 23:2). His tears reflect the genuine nature of his grief, going beyond the dutiful mourning expected of a husband in this ancient time and culture.

In spite of sorrow's pull, Abraham is able to resist. He has faithfully remained at his bride's side, lamenting his loss, but now he rises (v.3), intentionally stepping away from the grasp of grief. There is work to be done.

Even though God had promised Abraham Canaan, we realise that Abraham has not yet been given this inheritance (Acts 7:5). He owns no land, which means he has nowhere to bury Sarah. So, having risen from Sarah's side, he sets out to talk with the Hittites, seeking a plot of land with which to honour the matriarch of his family.

At the city gate, Abraham's humility leads him to first confess himself to be an alien and stranger among the Hittites (Genesis 23:4)—despite having lived among them for several decades—and then to bow down before them (vv.7 & 12). With great regard, Abraham acknowledges his place among the Hittites. He is not of their people and refuses to presume on their hospitality, yet he is in need of their generosity.

The Hittites' response reflects their respect for this "mighty prince" among them (v.5): They make multiple offers of the free use of burial chambers and even the gift of a field and cave (v.11). Their admiration of Abraham shines in every offer for him to bury his dead among their own.

Not wanting to risk future generations questioning this burial site's ownership, Abraham insists on paying for the field in Machpelah, affording us a glimpse of ancient Near Eastern culture where transactions such as this happened publicly and were sealed by words. Even as the transaction is secured, Ephron seems reluctant to discuss the price, saying, "But what is that between you and me?" (v.15), indicating that he values his relationship with Abraham more than money—a sure sign of respect.

Full of sorrow, Abraham buries his wife in the cave of Machpelah (v.19). His great loss motivates this man of God to purchase a field in a land that is not yet his own, and it becomes a downpayment of faith that one day God will fulfil His promise to him.

We can live in the same type of hope-giving faith. When we feel the weight of sorrow's pull, we can turn to our Father for help. Sitting in His presence and dwelling on His words of hope change us. When we recall His promises to be our strength (Philippians 4:13), to always be with us (Matthew 28:20), and to give us comfort (Matthew 5:4), we are supernaturally supported, able to rise up and keep moving forward in a faith that was paid for by our Redeemer, Jesus Christ.

Where do you need to allow yourself to feel sorrow's pull and create space to grieve? What might that look like, and how can you invite God into your mourning?

DAY TWENTY-EIGHT

What If?

EMILY TYLER

Genesis 24:1-27

At this point in Genesis, Abraham is reaching the end of his life, and concerned with the continuation of his family line, he charges a "senior servant" to find Isaac a bride in his home country (Genesis 24:2-4). While the servant in this passage is unnamed, we can assume that it is Eliezer, who has been with Abraham from the beginning of his call (Genesis 15:2-3). This mission is an extensive journey. As the crow flies, from Canaan to Ur of the Chaldeans is approximately 800 kilometres, but the most common route travelled at that time was a hefty 1,450 kilometres of circuitous roads.

Our faith journeys are also long with countless twists and turns. Multiple times I have uttered Eliezer's same words in response to God's call in my life: *"What if...?"*

"What if dropping out of university is the wrong decision?"

"What if moving to the other side of the world damages my kids in some way?"

"What if I'm not accepted?"

And the most common question, the one that lies deep in my heart but is rarely heard out loud: *What if I fail?*

Eliezer reminds us it's not wrong to ask questions of the mission set before us, but it's important that the questions don't stop us from going. It's been said that it's hard to steer a parked car; we need to be moving to receive the direction. And as we're being guided to God's appointed place, what comes out of our mouths after *what if?* sets the tone for the rest of the story.

Eliezer's prayer is time-sensitive, specific, and humble. Hunting for a bride with such nuanced requirements could easily take days, weeks, or even months, so he asks for God's help *today* (v.12), humbly requests success for the overwhelming mission, and asks that he will recognise the already-chosen wife God has appointed for Isaac (v.14).

We see this pattern of prayer mirrored when Jesus teaches the disciples how to pray (Matthew 6:9-13). In the Lord's Prayer, we ask for our daily bread, for the things we need in this moment, for this task, right now. When we ask for God's will to be done and His Kingdom to come, we can trust that God will reveal His purpose and plans for the specific situation or season we find ourselves in.

And "before he had finished praying, Rebekah came out" (v.15). *Before he finished!* We know that before we ever even mutter a word, the Lord knows what is on our minds and will answer (Isaiah 65:24). Not only does God answer before Eliezer has finished praying, but He also goes above and beyond. Rebekah is a virgin, beautiful, from the right family, has a servant heart, is kind, hospitable, and diligent. God takes Eliezer's prayer and does immeasurably more than requested. *Won't He do the same for us?* (Ephesians 3:20).

Eliezer faces doubt and concern in the face of such a monumental task, but his name means 'God is my help.' And despite having his 'what if' moment, he still sets out believing that God will fulfil and complete the task ahead.

Just as God led Eliezer on his journey, so, too, will He "make our paths straight" and lead us on ours as we trust and submit to Him in all our ways (Proverbs 3:5-6). He has not "abandoned his kindness and faithfulness to us" (Genesis 24:27), sending the Holy Spirit to guide and teach us (John 14:26), and as we continue on our long journeys, we will find that everything, including us, will be fulfilled and completed in Jesus (Colossians 2:10).

What are the 'what ifs' holding you back in this season? After you've identified them, stand and declare the Lord's prayer aloud. Invite His Kingdom rule into your heart that it might be in your life as it is in Heaven.

The Sojourner Is Seen

RACHEL LOUISE

Genesis 24:28-67

I'm often blown away when Scripture details the lives of those who would ordinarily be overlooked. This is where I sit up and pay attention because, if they're mentioned, there's something significant that *needs* to be seen, as in the journey of Abraham's humble servant.

As this unnamed man embarks on the task laid out before him, he petitions the Lord for success on his sojourn and that he would be led on the right road. He soon comes beside a spring, requesting a sign that will lead him to the right woman for his master's son. The original Greek word used for spring is *oir*, literally translating to 'the eye of the water.' And it is beside this 'eye' that the Lord deeply *sees* the servant. God's gaze delves beyond outward appearance to prayers made in the quiet of his heart which are answered even before they are through (v.45). Rebekah approaches, and the way ahead becomes clear. This resounding pattern of petition and answer blankets the entire journey as the servant asks for success (v.42) and sees it granted (v.56).

Under the Lord's gaze, the overlooked are seen. His faithful ones are answered and led on the right road. Twice God answers the servant's petition, and twice the servant responds to this grace in worship and thanksgiving. Upon meeting Rebekah, he "bowed down and worshipped the Lord" (v.48), and upon Rebekah's family approving her leaving with him, he "bowed down to the ground before the Lord" (v.52). His immediate response is one of prostration, of making himself physically low so that God may be lifted high.

Rather than taking success upon himself, glory is given to God alone.

This dramatic turn to worship doesn't just happen when the full journey is completed but at every successful step along the way. At every hurdle, the servant makes his petition, and at each victory, he gives thanks. The narrative is laced with God's divine guidance and faithfulness. And this sparkling testimony is what others see when they encounter him.

This entire endeavour is bursting with people seen by God—and made able to see each other. As Isaac looks up, he *sees* Rebekah (v.63), and Rebekah also looks up and *sees* Isaac (v.64). And so blossoms a marriage of being truly seen: a relationship of mutual love and comfort where he loves her and she comforts him (v.67).

By his witness of worship and testimony, the servant has thrown open the door between being seen by God and allowing God to be seen through him. In fact, the servant recounts the Lord's faithfulness for most of this chapter. His successful journey becomes a witness to the goodness of God, and Laban, known to have worshipped false gods, is shown what worshipping the one true God looks like.

This God-honouring success ultimately ends in Isaac and Rebekah being united, fulfilling Abraham's desire and God's promise that his offspring would increase—a promise sparking the lineage that will lead us to Jesus.

Like the unnamed servant, our own hearts are set on pilgrimage towards Christ. We lead lives of being seen by God and those who don't yet know Him. As we petition God for direction, we are led along the right road, and as we respond in worship, our lives become testimonies seen by those around us.

You are not beyond God's notice. And your seemingly small, everyday acts of obedience offer witness to those around you in ways you may never know. This is the glory of a quiet life, led by divine guidance and lived in a posture of worship: that as we are known by God, He may be known by others.

Where in your life have you not yet reached your desired destination? What progress and victories towards it could you stop and praise God for today? Thank Him that He sees you and will be faithful to outwork His plans and purposes for your life.

Persistent Prayer

TRISTANY CORGAN

Genesis 25

Twenty-six years ago, a young woman named Rebeka went to a doctor with symptoms of endometriosis, a uterine tissue disorder that can make it difficult for women to get pregnant. The doctor confirmed that she did indeed have endometriosis, but they also found something else: cancer. Thankfully, it was caught early, and a procedure was done to remove it. However, the damage caused would make it difficult for her to carry a baby in her womb. Doctors told Rebeka that she would likely not get pregnant, but if she did, there was only a small chance of carrying to term.

About five years later, Rebeka got married and tried getting pregnant, but as expected, there was no baby. The couple longed for a child for months without result, so they went to be prayed over by the elders of the church. That very weekend, she got pregnant. Nine months later, Rebeka gave birth to a healthy baby girl, and twenty years later that girl is honouring her with a devotion about the power of prayer.

My mother's story is similar to that of another woman who lived thousands of years ago and was also named Rebekah. This Rebekah was also unable to get pregnant and longing for a child. When we meet her in Genesis 25, her husband, Isaac, is praying to the Lord on her behalf (v.21). Isaac knows that God can work miracles. Forty years earlier, the Lord had enabled his barren, elderly mother, Sarah, to give birth to him (Genesis 21:1-7), and he trusts that God will do it again. And He does—Rebekah becomes pregnant as a result of Isaac's prayer and gives birth to twin boys (Genesis 25:24).

We are finite beings with limited power and limited control over what happens in our lives. But we serve an infinite, all-powerful, sovereign God who listens to our prayers and desires to give us good things (Matthew 7:11; James 1:17). Nothing is impossible with Him, for He is a miracle-working God (Matthew 19:26; Luke 1:37). He commands us to call out to Him about our needs, desires, concerns, and requests (Philippians 4:6). Our prayers change things! As James writes, "The prayer of a righteous person is powerful and effective" (James 5:16b).

But it doesn't always seem like it. Sometimes we pray and pray and pray, and nothing happens. However, just because we aren't seeing the answer we prayed for doesn't mean we should stop praying. Isaac was forty when he married Rebekah, and he is sixty when she gives birth (Genesis 25:20 & 26). *He prays for his wife for twenty years* before God finally gives them the children they have so longed for. Even if we've been praying for years, we must persist and heed Jesus' guidance: "Ask and it will be given to you; seek and you will find; knock and the door will be opened to you" (Matthew 7:7). Prayers that are months, years, or even decades old are still effective and powerful, so we must keep praying!

Just because we pray for something—even if we pray for a very long time— it doesn't mean we're guaranteed the results we hope for. But we can trust that God is sovereign, that He has a good plan for each of us (Romans 8:28), and that, as we pray, He will continually change our desires to make them more like His own (Romans 12:2). Rebekah, Isaac, and my parents persisted in their prayers for a child and trusted the Lord's timing, and their godly, righteous desires were finally met. Whatever is happening in your life, pray, pray, and pray some more. And trust that God knows what is best for you.

Is there anything or anyone that you have stopped praying for? Ask the Holy Spirit to kindle fresh hope to keep contending and spend some time right now praying for that situation.

A Spacious Place

EMILY TYLER

Genesis 26

As Abraham's promised heir, you might expect a significant amount of text in Genesis dedicated to Isaac's story, and yet we find very little. In many ways, his story mirrors Abraham's: a famine in the land, food and water in short supply, increased wealth through the Lord's blessing (v.12), lying about his wife being his sister, and now, insufficient room in his current location (v.16).

He has no place, no space, and no water.

In an agrarian culture like Isaac's, the nomadic lifestyle of moving to find appropriate pasture and water for your flocks was expected. Water was life. But the Philistines' envy at Isaac's wealth means all the wells his father had dug are now spitefully blocked up. So, he unexpectedly must move and set about the hard work of reopening the wells. No sooner do Isaac's servants discover fresh water for his flocks, however, than fallout with the nearby Gerar herders results in these wells being unavailable, too, and again, Isaac is forced to move on and dig new ones. If that wasn't frustrating enough, there is further trouble, and he must relocate and dig *again*.

Isaac goes from one location to the next, trying to find water—trying to find life—only to be met repeatedly with opposition, jealousy, and unkindness.

It would be natural for Isaac to want to demand that the Philistines move on and give back the wells that he is entitled to, to tell the herders to dig their own wells. But just as Isaac learned unhelpful traits from his father, he also learned the beauty of laying down his rights and choosing instead to trust God.

Isaac doesn't fixate on whether the opposition he faces is just. He doesn't whinge at the unfairness of having wells stolen from him during a famine. He doesn't refuse to dig more wells when the first few don't work out. He simply continues to trust God and faithfully does the next right thing.

Eventually, Isaac's resolute faithfulness pays off. He discovers fresh water and declares, "Now the Lord has given us room and we will flourish in the land" (v.22). God has made room—enlarged, expanded, and extended the space—for Isaac and his family to rest. He has brought them into a "spacious place" (Psalm 18:19), and He wants to do the same for us.

My own life often reflects Isaac's: desperate to find my own space in the crowd, squashed under the demands of daily living, feeling crushed when others are purposefully spiteful. All too frequently, I hunt for refreshment in the wrong places. Constantly looking to the next thing to give me life, I keep digging, but there's no water.

In parched and weary seasons, when we're looking at all the holes in our lives that are failing to provide the life-giving drink we need, or when all we see is opposition and oppression, it can be easy to wonder where God is in our wandering. But His promise to Isaac remains the same for us: "I will be with you and will bless you" (Genesis 26:3).

It is as we model our lives after Isaac's in faithfully trusting God through repetitive disappointments and setbacks that we discover the space, place, and living water we crave is found only in Him.

The Father calls us from our empty wells, "Come, all you who are thirsty, come to the waters" (Isaiah 55:1); Jesus whispers, "If only you knew, the water I give means you'll never thirst again" (John 4:10-14); and the Spirit beckons, "Let the one who is thirsty come; and let the one who wishes take the free gift of the water of life" (Revelation 22:17b).

This well will never run dry.

What does a 'spacious place' look like for you? Bring this desire before the Father and ask the Holy Spirit to show you what the 'next right thing' is for you to do to partner with Him in moving into this space.

In His Good Timing

ADÉLE DEYSEL

Genesis 27:1-29

In my teens, I received a promise from God that I would lead worship on an international stage. My excitement in knowing that God sees me faded as my limitations became my focus. Surrounded by talented musicians and vocalists, I felt my gifts lacked in comparison. I began looking to the world to accept me but instead felt invisible and overlooked. I was crushed. With everything inside me, I clung to my promise, but in the process, I lost sight of the Promise Giver.

In Genesis 25, while she is pregnant with twins, God says to Rebekah that "the older will serve the younger" (Genesis 25:23); it is a prophecy that contradicts the tradition of the birthright belonging to the eldest son. Rebekah and Jacob, her favourite son, later set out to attain the promise through deceit, tricking Esau into selling Jacob his birthright and Isaac into blessing him first. Then Jacob runs, leaving a trail of destruction behind and ahead of him.

The same rivalry we see in Isaac's family is often seen in God's family. When we build our life around a promise, it can lead to chasing our own idea of what it should look like. We risk compromising our character and values and can end up competing with one another to see our promise realised.

Jacob and Esau both have uniquely created destinies and will become great nations (Genesis 25:23), yet this promise is overshadowed as their lives revolve around the birthright-blessing. Our rivalry with others is often fuelled by what we believe to be the more important promise. When we turn our focus away from God and onto ourselves, division sets in, and we lose sight of the promised destiny for us all. Each of us has a 'birthright-blessing,' and we were created with the end—and the path to get there—already known to God (Ephesians 2:10). Forcing that promise into fulfilment, however, is not only unwarranted but also harmful, because it places the emphasis on the promise instead of the Promise Giver.

The value of a promise lies in the one that makes it, and God proves His faithfulness time and time again to Abraham and his family. If Rebekah and Jacob had only been patient and trusted God's timing, the outcome of their story could have been different. Jacob's price for his deceit is high and unnecessary; he would have received the blessing anyway, because God promised it.

God is faithful. I knew this in my own story, but discovering the reality of that truth came from being broken and lost as the process of immigrating to New Zealand caused me to question my purpose and identity. In our search for a new church, all I wanted was to blend in; I wanted my life to pass by as unnoticed as I felt. But in my darkest days, I desperately reached out to God and began to understand that I was known, accepted, chosen before I was created (Ephesians 1:4-6). As my dependence on God increased, so did my passion to serve Him. God, my Promise Keeper, set into motion the fulfilment of His promise for my life when He prompted me—at the right time, with the right heart—to join our worship team.

My identity had to be redefined before my promise was realigned.

God has uniquely predestined each of us, there is no need to strive and fight against each other (or ourselves) to accomplish it. Our focus should be on our personal relationship with God, grounding our identity in His unrivalled love. This will empower us to sincerely celebrate with others, even our 'rivals,' when they succeed.

God *will* fulfil His promise for our lives—in His good timing.

Is there anyone that you see yourself as being in competition with? Ask the Holy Spirit to show you what is fueling these feelings of insecurity and rivalry, then spend some time thanking God for the purposes He has for both of you.

Unlocking Abundance

JEFF MCKEE

Genesis 27:30-46

Esau comes from an amazing heritage, but all that is coming to him—both his material and spiritual inheritance—has just slipped between his fingers.

It's all Jacob's fault! "Look," he says. "He took away my birthright, and now look, he has taken away my blessing!" (v.36 NKJV).

Esau's solution is primitive but effective. *I'll just kill him*, he thinks. *That way, birthright and blessing will be freed up, and I can have what is mine.*

Fortunately, before he can act on his plan, his mother warns Jacob, who flees for his life.

Most of the issues in this family are rooted in a scarcity mindset, as well as reflecting Abraham's treatment of his sons generations earlier. Ishmael missed out; Isaac inherited all. Now the pattern is to repeat again—until Jacob's impudence and Esau's negligence coalesce to allow the chosen brother to be dispossessed by the one who is to be overlooked. Okay for Jacob, but Esau is out in the cold because apparently there is not enough to go around!

Christ's 'golden rule' (do unto others as you would have them do unto you), His summary of the Law as extravagantly loving God and our neighbour, and His invitation into an abundant life combine to shatter the validity of a worldview based on lack and competition for privilege. A 'Robin Hood' model for addressing inequity presumes this fallen world possesses all the resources available to right every wrong. Yes, it is the lesser of two evils, but it remains an earth-bound compromise, one that does not do justice to the lavish abundance of God's resources and His expansive heart toward humankind. Esau need not go without for Jacob to prosper.

We need a richer perspective than scarcity to recalibrate to what was originally intended—and blessing is the perfect tool for the job. Blessing draws from deep wells, uncorrupted by the fallout of Eden that dashed our expectations and lowered our hopes. Using deliberate and substantive words, Mum and Dad call forth resources from spiritual storehouses. Individually tailored and freshly prepared supplies enter the tangible world via angelic stairways (Genesis 28:12), taking root in the life of a child—even a prodigal on the run after short-sheeting his brother.

Blessing is a type of approval, like a last will and testament—but so much greater in substance and scope and alive in a way that no legal document can be. Rather than a single act at the end of life, blessing is a lifestyle of declared affirmation that actively passes on what we have attained, seen and unseen, so that our children can stand upon our shoulders and build a life from there. A blessing deficit is essentially neglect. If we don't bless properly, every generation starts from scratch, *and why would we want that?*

Things come to a head as Esau cries out: "Have you only one blessing, my father? Bless me—me also!" (v.38 NKJV).

Thankfully, even though he is acting outside of his social norm, Isaac blesses his other son, too. He has more to give than he had thought.

The result is transformational—both sons prosper! In fact, if we move ahead in the story, we find the two grown brothers giving to each other with the words, "I have enough," ringing on their lips (Genesis 33). Things have changed for the better, so much so that, by the end of his life, we find Jacob moving round the room blessing one son after another (Genesis 49), an imperfect shadow of our Heavenly Father who grants every spiritual blessing to every one of His children who come before Him.

There is more than enough to go around. We are God's agents tasked with unlocking abundance for our children—whether they be natural or spiritual—through the instrument He uses for the same purpose. It is time to rise up and bless the ones we love!

Where in your life do you have a scarcity mindset that tells you there is not enough for you or your loved ones? Ask the Holy Spirit to give you some Scriptures to replace that lie with God's truth and begin to daily declare His Word—His blessing—over your situation.

Stairways to Heaven

ASHLEY KELLY

Genesis 28

One of the most terrifying moments in my parenting life involved a very tall ladder, my husband, and our four-year-old son. My husband had the shock of a lifetime when he heard two simple, sweet words: "Hi, Daddy!" These words, normally welcomed and cherished by any parent, are the last thing you want to hear when you are on the roof of a two-storey building, knowing the only way up is the appropriately-sized ladder behind you.

How my child successfully climbed up there—while holding a ball, mind you—I have no idea. How it could have ended in tragedy, I am completely aware (and utterly thankful it did not). How I now view ladders has been forever changed, influenced by this one event.

I don't know if I can compare my experience with a ladder to Jacob's, but I am confident his experience left him forever changed, too. This is where the Lord meets him, reassures him of the promise that was first given to Abraham, and further promises to be with him wherever he goes (Genesis 28:13-15). Setting the stone as a pillar is a tangible way for him to acknowledge this change and to mark the place as special, as a place to be remembered and never thought of the same again. This is a sacred space where glimpses of Heaven and glimmers of deity have been revealed. More than a simple ladder, Jacob has been granted a revelation of the stairway to Heaven.

This idea is not unique to Jacob. In ancient mythology, gateways to the gods were common and often depicted as stairways. Towers were built with the purpose of housing these stairways, which provided access points for the gods to come down among the people to receive offerings and worship. One helpful picture of this ancient idea is that of Heaven being upstairs and the earth being downstairs, connected by these mythical stairways.

While my own ladder incident is limited in effectiveness to the three of us involved, Jacob's encounter is limitless in effectiveness because it points to something—*someone*—far greater: Jesus.

In John 1:51, Jesus reveals Himself to be the One upon whom the angels ascend and descend. *He* is the stairway to Heaven, our access point to God. Just as Romans 5:1-2 says: "Therefore, since we have been justified through faith, we have peace with God through our Lord Jesus Christ, through whom we have gained access by faith into this grace in which we now stand."

Jacob's awe and wonder of finding himself in the presence of God should be rivaled by our own awe and wonder of discovering that the presence of God now dwells within us through the power of the Holy Spirit (Ephesians 3:17; Romans 8:8-9). No longer must a gateway to Heaven be marked by a pillar, a tower, or a temple—for Christ, the stairway to Heaven Himself, lives within us through His Spirit. Now, *we* are the temple of the Holy Spirit, our lives set up as pillars marking the presence of God, each of us a stairway on which the lost can encounter Jesus.

That should make us wonder: *Are people changed after their encounters with us, just as Jacob was after his encounter in that sacred place?* Our neighbours, coworkers, and family members should see glimmers of Heaven as they watch our lives and listen to our words because we live as its representatives. They should see Jesus in us; His presence should be evident in our lives. May we live in such a way that points to the wonder of who He is and what He has done for us.

Spend some time meditating on the incredible truth that you are now God's temple. How does this impact your daily life? Ask God to fill you afresh with awe and wonder for the privilege of housing His Spirit.

Seen by God

NICOLE O'MEARA

Genesis 29

He looked up and noticed me. *Me!* One of the popular boys in junior high saw me walking in his direction and perked up: "Nicole!" He smiled and opened his arms as if to give me a hug. I stumbled a bit but willed my feet to move forward. My heart beat faster. He stepped closer until, with arms wide open, he walked right past me. I turned and watched as he hugged the girl behind me. In a flash, I understood. Behind me was a more popular Nicole. Pretending not to notice, I turned quickly and walked away before anyone noticed the heat of embarrassment creep into my cheeks. *I should've known.*

Similarly, Jacob doesn't see Leah—doesn't even notice her, actually. Genesis 29:17-18 says it like it is: "Leah's eyes were weak, but Rachel was beautiful in form and appearance. Jacob loved Rachel." There are numerous ways we could read this description of Leah. 'Weak eyes' could mean she doesn't see well; it could describe the colour or shape of her eyes; or it could describe a less than sparkly personality. Regardless of the meaning, though, according to the standards of her day, Leah doesn't rate—and she knows it.

Still unmarried and living at home, Leah endures the pain of watching her younger sister draw the attention of Jacob. In further humiliation, Leah's father uses her to manipulate Jacob, trading her for Rachel on their wedding night (vv.23-25). The next morning, when Jacob finds Leah in bed beside him, he is outraged. He had fallen in love with Rachel the moment he saw her at the well (v.10-11) and then spent seven long years working unpaid for the privilege of making her his wife. He does not want Leah—he wants Rachel! Once again, Leah is overlooked, unprotected, and rejected.

If I had lived in Leah's day, I likely would have been overlooked, too. I have poor eyesight and wore ugly glasses as a child (there are much cuter options nowadays). I'm short, reserved, and just not as charismatic as some. After years of feeling overlooked, I began to believe I wasn't worthy of being noticed. I hid my body inside oversized clothes and my true sensitive personality inside that of an overlooked person. I moved as if I were invisible, avoiding people and hoping they would avoid me. In a weird way, I enjoyed being overlooked because it protected me from the discomfort of accidentally thinking someone noticed me, like that day in junior high. It's a sad way to live.

Leah shows us a better way. She is treated poorly, yet when she names her first son Reuben, which means "because the Lord has seen my misery," Leah reveals a heart comforted by God who knows her pain (v.32). She understands that God sees her even though the people around her don't.

Jacob overlooks Leah, and in the process, he misses something great: Leah's tremendous faith. Instead of living crushed because she is not loved by her father or her husband, Leah chooses to believe *God* loves her and has a good plan for her. And He does! God gives Leah, not Rachel, the privilege of beginning the line of Israel's kings through her son, Judah—a royal line that includes King David, and eventually, King Jesus.

Our God is *El Roi*, the God who sees (Genesis 16:13; Matthew 6:26); God saw Leah, and He sees each one of us. His love for us is higher and longer and wider and deeper than we can imagine (Ephesians 3:18). He is a good Father with a good plan for our lives. When we learn to see ourselves as He does, we find the confidence we need to live out those plans.

Invite the Father to show you how He sees you. What words and images does He bring to mind? Are there any changes you need to make in light of this renewed perspective?

Greater Trust, Greater Joy

CARA RAY

Genesis 30:1-24

It had been several years of trying unsuccessfully to conceive, and I had spent a small fortune on pregnancy tests. Each month, that single line seemed to mock me, reminding me that I was *still* without a child. I wrestled with why God had given me such a strong desire to be a mom and yet withheld the gift of children from me. I wondered if I would be able to praise God even if His answer to my heart's desire remained 'no.'

It's natural to desire children. However, this section of Scripture adds a layer of complexity to the struggle to start a family: the competition of another wife—and a sister, no less. Rachel has always been the love of Jacob's life, but her older sister, Leah, has been given to Jacob to marry first (Genesis 29:23-27). While Jacob doesn't hide his favouritism of Rachel, she remains childless, while her rival has many sons (vv.31-35).

Rachel is keenly aware of God's promises to Jacob's grandfather, Abraham. She knows a great nation will proceed from Jacob's loins. But the way things are going, she might be questioning if *she* will bear any of those offspring herself. Her desperation is clear when we find her in Genesis 30, crying out to Jacob, "Give me children, or I'll die!" (v.1). What started as a healthy desire has become Rachel's all-consuming passion.

Jacob, frustrated with her preoccupation with having a child, is now angry with Rachel, and he reminds her that giving children is God's business, not his, saying, "Am I in the place of God, who has kept you from having children?" (v.2). If God is in control of the womb, the obvious conclusion to draw is that Rachel needs to continue to wait patiently.

However, the reminder she needs most is the advice she outright rejects: Instead of waiting patiently, Rachel takes matters into her own hands. Just as Sarah gave Abraham Hagar to bear his child, Rachel gives Jacob her handmaid, Bilhah. *What could possibly go wrong?*

Rachel's plan appears successful when Bilhah gives birth to two sons, yet she is still not happy. The names she gives the boys reveal her heart. First, Dan is born, whose name means 'he has vindicated' (v.6), then Naphtali, whose name means 'my struggle' (v.8). Some time later, God finally gives

Rachel her heart's desire: a son whom she bears herself. She names him Joseph. But even after receiving this longed-for gift, her heart is still not satisfied; his name means 'may he add another' (v.24).

Rachel has missed the most important lesson of all: to praise God both in the waiting for and in the joyful receiving of her long-awaited son. With a newborn baby cradled in her arms, she still worries about a child she doesn't yet have.

Like Rachel, my years of longing for a child were finally fulfilled. While I wasn't competing for my husband's love and attention, I did learn that God was competing for mine. My waiting taught me to trust Him more and resulted in greater joy when it was finally time to receive.

Are you waiting on God to fulfil the desires of your heart? Can you trust that His will, done in His way, is better than any plans you can concoct on your own? That might seem like Jacob's reminder to Rachel right now: words you need but don't want to hear. But trust Him to fulfil your heart's desires, in His timing, in His way. When God Himself, and not His gifts, are our all-consuming passion, we will find joy in the waiting *and* in the receiving.

Is there anything God has been speaking to you that you haven't wanted to hear? What might it look like for you to heed His words today?

Out-of-the-Box Solutions

JEFF MCKEE

Genesis 30:25-43

We get mixed messages about wealth. If you have plenty, that's a mark of God's favour. If you are having it tough, avoid a money focus at all costs! Here, in the second half of Genesis 30, God's Word addresses that tension.

This part of Jacob's story follows hard on the heels of his family and responsibilities growing out of hand. Suddenly, he has lots of mouths to feed, his expenses are climbing fast, and his employer continually trims his wages rather than giving him a much-needed raise (Genesis 31:7).

With the significant material success of his father and grandfather snapping at his heels, he works as an employee shepherding his father-in-law's flocks. Everything benefits Laban, and Jacob is left living hand to mouth, with a singular question on his mind: *When will I provide for my own house?* (Genesis 30:30).

When we, too, take stock, and then exclaim, *What about me?* we ask a legitimate and biblical question. When the status-quo is broken and oppressive, it is okay to be dissatisfied.

There was a time when I was in a fairly dark place, struggling to provide for our family. It drove me to praying a Hannah-like prayer: "Lord, if you will take away my shame around a hopeless career, I will give it all back to you!" What came next was an extraordinary redemption of that area of my life. So extreme was God's intervention that I was left worshipping, unable to take any credit for what was undeniably an act of God.

Here in Genesis, God will take credit for sorting out Jacob's financial woes, as well. In fact, we only need to wait for the next chapter; it is in God's character to deliver swift justice to the needy.

It all starts when Jacob makes an observation (vv.37-39). From within the circumstances that bind him, he is provided a key to his release when he observes a specific set of conditions that greatly increases the flock's propensity to breed. God gives him a secret means of fruitfulness!

I imagine his elation as hope dawns on his frustrated mind. He finds the best and strongest animals in the flock and sets them in position to breed more, hoping to both increase the overall condition of the animals under his care and to increase their numbers. However, he uncovers two show-stoppers. Firstly, if the flock numbers increase out of hand, he won't have helped himself at all; Laban will prosper. Secondly, his stock numbers are improving but at the detriment of their overall physical appearance. The culture of his time valued unblemished colour, but speckled and striped sheep were popping up left and right, seemingly out of nowhere. Back to square one!

Then he has a divinely inspired idea (vv.40-42). One that is a challenge to follow him in as we live in a generation particularly fixated on Insta-worthiness and outward appearance.

What if he didn't care what everyone else thought? What if he prized what others most rejected? The animals were still strong and healthy, and it made no difference to the taste of their meat.

As Jacob affirms the revelation and adapts until he is completely in line with the fullness of God's will for him, we find him making a deal with Laban: *"You take the animals with solid colour that everyone prefers, and I'll take the ones you don't want with marks and blemishes."* His key is now fitted into a lock, and the Lord is able to prosper him.

It all begins with getting real about the things in our lives that aren't right. God has answers, and we can walk out of difficulty if we ignore the pressure to be shaped by our culture and instead remain open to out-of-the-box solutions.

What in your life isn't working? Carve out some time to strategise about these things with the Holy Spirit. What keys and insights is He showing you?

When It's Time to Go

CARA RAY

Genesis 31:1-21

We couldn't shake our feelings of restlessness. After countless hours of talking, praying, and weighing all the factors, we decided it was time for our family to make a fresh start in a new state. But almost as soon as the decision was made, we started to experience major roadblocks. We thought we were walking in obedience—*why was it so hard? Had we misunderstood the Lord?* We couldn't see it then, but God was making a way—we just had to wait for the right timing.

Jacob is in a similar situation in Genesis 31. For twenty years, he has faithfully served his uncle, Laban. But the temperature of the relationship has cooled, and Jacob overhears his cousins complaining that he has gained his wealth illegitimately from their father. The Lord confirms it is time to move on, telling him, "Go back to the land of your fathers and to your relatives, and I will be with you" (v.3).

Six years earlier, Jacob had tried to leave at the end of his initial contract, but Laban knew the Lord was blessing him because of Jacob and begged him to stay (Genesis 30:27). Now, the situation is different: God is making a way for Jacob to go back to the land of his forefathers—but that doesn't mean it will be easy to cut ties with his uncle.

As Jacob discusses the move with his wives, he recounts how God has blessed and prospered his service: When Laban offered Jacob the speckled lambs for payment, the flocks produced more speckled, and when he offered him the streaked lambs, the flocks bore more streaked . A miracle! Regardless of Laban's antics, God faithfully sees to it that Jacob's household prospers. But this should come as no surprise to Jacob, for this is exactly what God said to him at Bethel.

Years earlier, God promised Jacob in a dream that He would give him land, descendents, and make his seed a blessing (Genesis 28:13-14). He even promised Jacob he would not be alone, assuring him, "I am with you and will watch over you wherever you go, and I will bring you back to this land. I will not leave you until I have done what I have promised you" (v.15). Jacob also made a vow to God, declaring that if God would go with him and provide all that he needed, then the Lord would be his God (v.20).

Now it is time for Jacob to act on what he promised. God is making a way, and He has provided all that Jacob has needed in the past. The question is, *will Jacob trust Him in all the uncomfortable parts of the journey that lies ahead?*

When life transitions happen, we should expect our faith in God to be stretched. That was certainly our experience when we felt God moving us to a new state. We did eventually get there, but it wasn't in the timeframe we anticipated. Now in hindsight, we can see His timing was better than our own, and it grew our faith and trust in Him in the process.

When it's time for you to move on, you can trust God to speak and direct your steps. Jacob knew God would eventually return him to his homeland—it was just a matter of timing. And just as God promised Jacob that he would be with him wherever he went, He will be with you also. No matter where you reside, if you have the God of Abraham, Isaac, and Jacob going with you, you are never alone—and that is the greatest reassurance of all!

Where is God stretching your faith right now? How is He inviting you to trust Him more in this time? Take a moment to thank Him for the gift of His faithful presence as you navigate this transition.

Finishing Well

ANYA MCKEE

Genesis 31:22-55

The latter half of Genesis 31 is, if nothing else, the story of a family in transition. Jacob, his two wives, and their respective children, along with an amassed hoard of livestock, have decided it's time to relocate. In fact, they're going home—at least, it's home for Jacob. His two wives have probably never ventured outside of Paddan-Aram, but they've made their own family now; they travel as a pack.

I know the feeling of leaving one country to travel to another. It's a mission, getting everything packed, the goodbyes said, the last memories made, the logistics of it all....

Jacob and his wives didn't bother with too much of that, though. It intrigues me that they managed to keep the whole thing a secret, to the point where Laban goes off to shear his sheep and returns three days later to find they essentially up and left the minute he was out of sight (vv.19-21).

Something about their manner of leaving seems out-of-kilter. *Jacob takes another man's daughters away without so much as a farewell kiss? He leaves an employer after twenty years without even a handshake? He decides what's his to take without even the courtesy of a discussion?*

Laban has done plenty wrong by Jacob, but he is still his father-in-law, still the grandfather of his children, still the one who agreed to hire him in the first place. It is Laban's home Jacob is leaving, Laban who will have to pick up the slack when he finds them gone. God is repositioning Jacob for blessing, but in so doing, Laban's been left in the lurch.

If there's anything I've learned in life's transitions, it's this: Finishing well matters. Most of all, relationships matter. It's okay to move when God says move; it's even okay to move quickly when He says move quickly. But in all the obedience, the hearing and heeding the word of the Lord, the life-altering steps of faith, it's worth pausing a moment to remember that our decisions don't only affect us. There are others in the mix—most notably, those we leave behind.

And so, I've learned to safeguard the leaving. Whether we're starting a new job or moving into a new neighbourhood, I say a simple prayer: "Whenever it's time to move on, I pray we will do so with every relationship intact." It's a prayer God cares deeply about because He cares deeply about people.

God wants Jacob and his family to enjoy the season ahead, but He knows Jacob will never fully settle if he's constantly worried that Laban will turn up riled. There's nothing like unfinished business or fractured relationships to dampen the joy of an otherwise glorious new season.

And so, true to character, God intervenes to bring things back on track.

As Laban sets out in pursuit of his son-in-law, the Lord personally advises him not to speak a word to Jacob, either good or evil, when they meet (v.24). Laban tries his best, but it's inevitable—tensions are high on both sides. Both men are trying to hold back, to keep their calm, but there's twenty years of pent-up angst between them, and it's not easy to navigate in the moment.

Finally, they realise that finishing well is in everyone's interest, that families matter, and traditions matter, and feasting matters. And so they build a memorial, offer a sacrifice, and gather one last time to share a meal.

In the morning, there are proper goodbyes, and we breathe a sigh of relief. They've managed to finish well! This is God at His finest—releasing people into their destinies with every relationship intact.

What a privilege it is to partner with God in this. Even so, the anticipation and practicalities as we step into a new season can be all-consuming. Let's not be so intent on following God's leading that we neglect to finish well with those who are often most impacted by our obedience—the ones we leave behind.

Is there anywhere in your life where you don't feel you've 'finished well'? Ask the Holy Spirit to show you how you can still show honour to the people and places of your past.

While We Wait

NICOLE O'MEARA

Genesis 32:1-21

For three tense days, I waited in the hospital while a surgeon made careful preparations for a risky surgery to save my life. This time was needed to assemble the best team and eliminate as many variables as possible; the wait was excruciating, but it was necessary for my good.

While we waited, my husband and I hoped for the best and prepared for the worst. We also did one more thing: We prayed. We prayed weak, humble prayers admitting our fears and gripping tightly to our faith in God. That may seem contradictory, but reading about Jacob's second stressful moment in the desert assures me that it is not.

The first time Jacob camped in the desert, he was fleeing for his life, running away from Esau's anger (Genesis 28). This time, in Genesis 32, he's walking straight into a potentially deadly encounter with his brother. The first time, Jacob didn't trust God, and his modus operandi was deception. This time, he has a budding trust relationship with God, and his MO is changing; he's becoming more forthright. While still a work in progress, he's learning what it means to be a dependent child of God and to take steps of faith despite his fears.

It's his response to the news that Esau is coming—with four hundred men— that reveals this maturing faith. Jacob is initially "in great fear and distress" (v.7), but instead of returning to his old tricks, Jacob's first response is to pray. He prays a simple, genuine prayer recalling God's promises, confessing his dependence on God, and specifically requesting God's action on his behalf. Then, Jacob prepares. He methodically separates his herds, sending a large number ahead as a gift, with a humble message honouring Esau. His elaborate gifts reveal a heart ready to reconcile with his brother and a willingness to do what is within his power to make that possible.

Jacob prays, prepares, and then he waits, spending the night alone in the camp while everyone else sets out to meet Esau. In past moments of stress, Jacob has taken impulsive action to secure God's blessings and establish himself (Genesis 27:5-29); this time, he is patiently confident. He trusts that God has heard his prayers and will take care of him, no matter the outcome of his meeting with his brother.

Learning to trust God with our fears doesn't happen overnight. Like any new skill, waiting well takes practice, and while we may not always get it right, with time, our faith grows. Paul David Tripp writes, "Waiting is not just about what I get at the end of the wait, but about who I become as I wait." Waiting three days for my surgery revealed what was in my heart: a lot of fear and a lot of faith. The wait also produced in me a deeper reliance on God. I learned to come near to Him for comfort and to place my fears in His hands. When I was back in surgery nine months later, that deeper reliance on God was visible to others. The anesthesiologist, who had been with me in the first surgery, placed his hand on my shoulder and said, "You're different. You look more at peace."

Life will inevitably bring seasons of waiting. Jacob's wait reminds us that waiting provides space for the transformative work of the Holy Spirit to take place in our hearts. Seasons of waiting can be great opportunities to partner with God in the strengthening of our faith—if we allow them to be.

Reflect on your own seasons of waiting. What has God taught you in them? Which of these lessons do you need to hold onto in your present places of waiting?

DAY FORTY-ONE

Daring to Grapple

JENNA MARIE MASTERS

Genesis 32:22-32

When my son was just four months old, I found out I was pregnant again. I was so surprised—another baby! But when we saw two babies instead of one floating on the ultrasound screen, I was shocked: *Twins!*

Then one night, after pricing triple strollers online, I started to bleed. The doctor told me I was miscarrying one of my babies and that there was nothing I could do—but I knew he was wrong.

I *could* go to God for comfort; I *could* ask my Heavenly Father for peace and for Him to carry my baby home in His loving hands. But I was hurt and confused. I wasn't ready to fall into His arms. I didn't want Him to take my baby anywhere without me. Oh, I wanted my God to show up, but it was so I could offer up fistfuls of questions and heartache. My spirit was in turmoil. This daughter needed to wrestle with her Father.

God welcomes our need to wrestle. There is no form of battle more intimate. It's grabbing hold, skin-to-skin, breath-to-breath, strength against strength. As Jacob describes it in this passage, it is a "face to face" experience (Genesis 32:30).

Jacob's wrestling with God isn't merely physical. Jacob must have questions, lying alone the night before he is to face his brother: *Why had Laban deceived him? Why would God lead him to Esau, who will surely kill him?!*

But God doesn't come with answers. He comes with a wrestling mat and invites Jacob to sprawl his unmet expectations out on the sweaty, sticky floor and bring it. *Why?* Because God desires intimacy. He is Immanuel, the God who wants to be with Jacob. The God who wants to be with us, to be known by us. Our God would rather us run to Him with fists in the air than run from Him hoarding questions we're too afraid to ask.

We desire to be known, too, because He formed us in His image—inviting us to press in and fight for intimacy. But sometimes we walk away from this fellowship, chasing lies instead.

Maybe we pridefully believe our plans are better than His. At times, we hold a muddled conception of God's character; we believe the lie, "God isn't always good," and our path to intimacy gets clogged. *Because if God isn't always good, why would we trust Him not to harm us in our vulnerability?* Or perhaps we think God isn't interested in hearing about our heartache because He's consumed with bigger things.

God's Word combats these lies: "'For I know the plans I have for you,' declares the Lord, 'plans to prosper you and not to harm you, plans to give you hope and a future. Then you will call on me and come and pray to me, and I will listen to you'" (Jeremiah 29:11-12). God's plans are good, and He will not harm us. He will listen to us.

If we choose to walk away from God in our struggles, we miss the chance to see His face. We miss opportunities for God to refine us. God didn't wrestle with Jacob to crush his spirit but to clarify his identity (v.28). And He wants to do the same for all His children.

Those who dare to grapple with God dare to know Him. The night we 'lost' one of our twins remains one of the most intimate moments I've spent with Jesus. I came at Him full force with every emotion imaginable. *And you know what I found?*

A God who stayed—Immanuel, God with me.

Jesus has proved over and over that He will never leave, even in the most honest, grisly moments. He welcomes our questions and doubts (Luke 7:20-21). Let us be like Jacob, willing to wrestle so we can fully embrace the God who passionately wants to know us.

What do you need to dare to grapple with God over? Create space for this: write a letter, take a prayer walk, paint, cry, yell—be as creative as you like, but do what it takes to open the door of communication between you and the Lord. How could you create space for this?

The Road to Reconciliation

AMBER PALMER

Genesis 33

The road to reconciliation can be long and hard. As someone who is still dealing with a situation that happened years ago, I continue to wrestle with my feelings about the person who brought pain, disappointment, and heartache into my life. Their mistakes pushed my family abruptly down a road we never expected. Yet when I think back to this season, the emotions associated with this person are no longer as raw as they were when I was first wronged by them.

Allowing God to do a good work in our heart is a process. It often takes time for our decision to forgive to be heartfelt, for us to completely surrender our hurts and for the sting to go out of them. We see this modelled for us in Jacob's relationship with his brother, Esau.

I can't help but picture the meeting of Jacob and Esau in Genesis 33 as though it were the climatic scene in a movie. This would be the moment the viewers would be waiting on the edge of their seats as the brothers are about to come face-to-face. *Will Jacob get what he deserves after his deceptive ways?* We expect an epic fight scene, but instead a 'but God' moment unfolds on the broken road of their life when Esau runs to meet Jacob and "embraced him and fell on his neck and kissed him, and they wept" (v.4).

During the twenty years Jacob and Esau have spent apart, God has softened their hearts, allowing the narrative to shift. We see a transition from death to life and the miracle of a relationship restored with God's help. Jacob, who once looked out only for himself, is now bowing before his brother not once, but seven times with prepared gifts. This is a sign of respect and honour and shows how Jacob's heart toward Esau has changed, as well as his willingness to take ownership of his actions. Esau may have been the one who runs to embrace Jacob, but *together* they weep. Jacob weeps from the heaviness of his own sin and relief at its resolution; it is in this moment that he receives forgiveness from Esau, as well as from God Himself.

Time doesn't always heal all wounds, but it can give the space we need to bring perspective and clarity into challenging situations. It can dampen our fleshly desires and the urge to resolve things our way and in our power. When we take our need for control, revenge, or to be right out of the problem and allow God an opening to do the hard heart work, there is an opportunity for transformation to take place like it did with Jacob and Esau.

Forgiveness, and even reconciliation, does not always mean that relationships go back to the way they were before they were fractured. Like Esau and Jacob going their separate ways, sometimes God may lead us to forgive and then maintain distance or put boundaries in place; other times, connection is fully restored. But regardless of the outcome, forgiveness is always an act of obedience to God and an expression of our devotion to Him; we forgive because He forgave us (Colossians 3:13).

It is only through God that a hate as strong as Esau's and sin as deep as Jacob's could be brought to a place of restoration; only through Him healing could come out of pain and deception. And it is only through Jesus, our prepared gift, that forgiveness is promised, mending the divide between us and God. When we give space and open ourselves up to obedience, we can trust God to bring forth forgiveness in our hearts and to right the wrongs against us.

Is there any way in which you are holding on to unforgiveness? Invite the Holy Spirit to come alongside you, both to empower the decision to forgive and to minister to you as your Comforter and Counsellor.

God Will Judge

ELLIE DI JULIO

Genesis 34

The story of Dinah is difficult to read, full of degradation, violence, arrogance, and sin bordering on blasphemy. There is no way to read it and not feel the grief of God.

Yet where is God in this narrative? Although this chapter is sandwiched between others rich with His presence, His absence is tangibly felt as we watch Dinah's debasement at Shechem's hands, her brothers' abuse of the covenant sign of circumcision, the dishonourable slaughter and sacking of a city, and Jacob's confrontation with the ringleaders—his sons, Simeon and Levi. The chapter then ends abruptly in disgrace for everyone involved; there is no resolution.

Our soul cries out against these perversions of justice escalating from a woman's defilement to the fracturing of a nation. We're left aching for the Lord to intervene somewhere, anywhere, and make it right—to hand down judgement, not only for Dinah's trauma but also for the people of Shechem, ignobly murdered and enslaved, and for the family of Israel, poisoned by the bitter fruit of pride.

The good news is that God *is* here, and He *does* make it right. But as is so often the case, God's justice is not quite what we expect.

Our vengeful flesh thrills at the destruction of Shechem in retaliation for Dinah's violation, edified by what the perpetrators reap from sowing manipulation, cruelty, and insolence. Simeon and Levi lose their inheritance as their father curses their sin on his deathbed, their tribes and lands stripped from them and their descendants (Genesis 49:5-7). Here, they pay the price for usurping God's right to judge Shechem by disappearing from the story of Israel (Deuteronomy 18:1; 33).

To us, this seems just punishment. But because God's justice is not the same as ours, it isn't where the story ends. The God of Israel is merciful and long-suffering, desiring all His children be reconciled to Him (1 Timothy 2:1-6). Which is why Jesus didn't merely come to redeem the people who came after Him but *all humanity across all time* (Romans 8:38-39; 1 Peter 3:18-19).

Reading on to Revelation, we find that Simeon and Levi are included in the list of those sealed for the glory of the Living God in the final days (Revelation 7:4-8). All twelve tribes of Israel—all twelve sons—are represented without exception.

The proud are humbled. The lost are found. Those who sinned are forgiven. We aren't told how or why—yet it is.

And while we may balk at the wicked being saved, let us not forget that we are as guilty as Simeon, Levi, *and* Shechem (Romans 3:23). We may not have razed a city or ravaged an innocent, but Jesus said if we are even angry with someone, we sin and are subject to judgment as if we had committed murder (Matthew 5:21-22). And who in their life has not been angry with not just one person but *entire groups of people?* The conviction is enough to bring anyone to their knees—which is exactly where we belong, first in grief, then in worship and praise.

God is not absent in the story of Dinah. He is there, in her very name: *judgment*, or more aptly, *God will judge*. And He does just that. As prophesied and promised across the whole of Scripture, God's justice ensures the guilty are disciplined. But His mercy also offers the opportunity for redemption. If God has extended His love and forgiveness across millennia to redeem the many sins of Simeon and Levi, how great is our assurance that Jesus extends that same love and forgiveness to us here and now, in our sin-ravaged past, and for all time.

Where in your life do you need to trust God for justice? As things come to mind, write them down, then write "God Will Judge" across each one as a statement of trust in His ability to balance the justice and mercy required.

A New Name

NICOLE O'MEARA

Genesis 35

When we adopted our son and daughter from a foreign country, we were given the choice to rename them. We wanted new names to symbolise our intentional choice to claim them as our own, but also wanted to honour their heritage. So we decided to keep our children's original names chosen by their birth parents as their middle names and gave them new first names.

However, this created a challenge.

Our adopted son was old enough to know his birth name and learning his new name wasn't easy. He didn't speak English, and we didn't speak his language. So, for about a year, we said his first and middle names together. His face told us exactly what he was thinking: *Who are these people, and why do they keep saying my name wrong?* So, we made it fun by giving him treats when we said his name. "Steven William*, look here" —treat. "Steven William, taste this" —treat.

Our desire was for our son to learn to identify us as his parents, to trust us to provide for him, and to identify with his new family. In essence, every time we said his name, we sent a message: *This thing we are doing when we feed you and put you to sleep near us and help you get dressed is called being a family. And we will keep doing this forever.*

We knew what our son didn't. He was no longer an orphan; we were now his parents. He no longer needed to find his own food; we would feed him. He no longer needed to live in fear; we would keep him safe. He had a new family, a new identity, and a new future. It took time and repetition for him to adjust to his new name and new situation, but he did.

I thought of my son's struggle as I read Genesis 35:10: "'Your name is Jacob, but you will no longer be called Jacob; your name will be Israel.'" God has already given Jacob his new name back in Genesis 32, but He knows what Jacob doesn't: Big challenges are ahead, and Jacob will need to know the truth of who he is.

Jacob is about to face intense grief. He will have to grieve the death of his beloved wife (v.18), the betrayal of his firstborn son (v.22), and finally the death of his father (v.29). To prepare him for the challenges ahead, God reminds Jacob of his identity. When God speaks his new name, *Israel* (meaning "God contends"), He is sending a message: *"Remember who you are. I have chosen you and I will contend for you."* Jacob will not need to resort to his old methods of deception to fight for himself. As Israel, he can trust God Almighty for care and protection and can lean on Him for strength and comfort during a very challenging time.

Our birth names are a reflection of where we come from. The hope that we have as Christians is that, whether our heritage feels beautiful or otherwise, we also now bear a God-given name. In times of great challenge, we need to remember who we are in Christ. As adopted children, we are called *chosen* by God (Ephesians 1:3-4) and *share in the rich inheritance* that belongs to all God's children (Colossians 1:10-14). Nothing we do and nothing done to us can threaten our status as a *beloved child of God* (Romans 8:38-39). Our future is *secure* because our names are written in God's Book of Life and cannot be scratched out (Revelation 3:5). We will *never be forgotten*, for our names are tattooed on the palm of God's hand (Isaiah 49:15-16)!

May we daily lean into the rich blessing and security of our God-given name.

God calls us by many names. Take a moment to ask Him in prayer which name He has for you in this particular season. What is it and how does it reflect your true identity in Him?

*Names changed to protect privacy.

Building a Dynasty

ANYA MCKEE

Genesis 36

The genealogy of Esau is, at best, completely unremarkable. It seems there's nothing here—just the barest details of a man's family tree. Like a ghost town with tumbleweed drifting through, it's the absence of anything noteworthy in Esau's legacy that is most striking.

What an insipid lineage! While other individuals feature throughout Scripture, their lives woven into a grand story, the descendants of Esau seem disconnected from the bigger picture, isolated from their wider family; it's as if they've slipped into obscurity and are largely ignored in the biblical narrative. Sure, their names are recorded, but from the divine perspective, it's as if there is little more to add.

Is there really no glory, no greatness, no victories to be found among the succeeding generations of a man who once was directly in line to inherit all of the blessings and promises given to Abraham?

There's no doubt Esau is a hard-working man; he's accumulated plenty of possessions—so much so that the land he shares with his brother can no longer sustain both families. You'd think, given that he has already surrendered his birthright to his brother (Genesis 25:34) and lost his blessing to him as well, that Esau might at least contend for the land— perhaps suggest that his brother leave and let him stay. Surely Esau wants to hang onto *something* of his heritage.

But herein lies the issue: Esau has never valued his inheritance, never truly owned the promises of his mother and father. It began when he turned a blind eye to their desire for him to marry a woman of their own tribe and instead took two Hittite women as wives. Genesis 26 tells us they were "a source of grief" to Isaac and Rebecca (v.35).

When it comes to family and legacy, Esau just doesn't seem to care. He doesn't care about his birthright, his choice of wife, or even the opinion of his parents. He has little thought for anyone but himself and his immediate needs.

The problem is, we can't establish a dynasty on such short-lived, self-centred desires. It's all up for grabs unless we take hold of the promises and prophecies that God has for each one of us. In the moments when we're desperate or worn down or hankering for an easy answer to a pressing situation, we need to take stock. There's more at stake than meets the eye. It's not just about us. It's not just a moment in time. The value we place on things today has the potential to reach far into the future—to impact generations to come, to set our descendants up either for influence or for insignificance.

In our family, we started talking in terms of 'dynasty' quite a few years ago. It's been challenging to set aside our immediate needs to focus on one, two, even three generations ahead. *How do you live intentionally for people who you have not met, grandchildren and great-grandchildren who are yet to exist?* Esau's desire for instant gratification plays out in a moment and impacts hundreds of years that follow. An inter-generational mindset takes the opposite stance: To set up what's to come, we must sacrifice a little now. To ensure those who come after us enjoy Heaven's attention and affirmation, we must capture a vision that reaches beyond the here and now; we must set our eyes on things above, value God's will, and yield to His preferences. In so doing, we can turn a moment of focus into a lifestyle and a lifestyle into a legacy.

What is your vision for the future generations? What is one thing you could start to do to sow into that vision?

What's My Destiny?

MAZHAR KEFALI

Genesis 37

I love the movie *Forrest Gump*. Such a loveable character who sees the world so innocently and sincerely. He has one big life question: "Momma, what's my destiny?" Later, standing at the graveside of his beloved Jenny, he asks, "Are we floating around on the breeze, accidental-like? Momma says we make our own destiny. Maybe it's both?"

Like Forrest, we all want to know why we are here.

As the Genesis story unfolds, we meet the fourth patriarch, Joseph. While we are told that "this is the account of Jacob" (v.2), it occurs through the eyes and journey of Joseph, reflecting the biblical worldview that life is lived out through the family generationally.

Joseph's story provides a window into how God reveals and shapes a person's 'destiny.' It's not floating in the breeze, not an accident, and ultimately, isn't determined by us. His life reveals the amazing, sovereign grace of God, inviting us to see the supreme artist at work as He weaves together Joseph's destiny; God takes all of his choices and the actions of others in his life and working them together to form a God-honouring young man who becomes a blessing to an entire nation (Genesis 50:20; Romans 8:28f). It is perhaps the most profound illustration in Scripture of how God works providentially in the lives of His children.

But Joseph's life is anything but plain sailing. His father creates conflict between him and his brothers by marking him out as the favoured son (vv.3-4). He gives him, the youngest, "a richly ornamented robe," a counter-cultural choice. The giving of a robe in that time signified identity and a position of honour and favour, indicating the chosen son who would most likely receive the double portion inheritance and lead the next generation. Because of his love for Rachel, Jacob chooses Joseph, her first born but second-to-last of Jacob's children, over Reuben, Leah's eldest and the firstborn of all. The brothers know exactly what this means—hence the jealousy and outright hatred.

Not only does Joseph's earthly father set him apart with favour, so does his Heavenly Father, giving him two dreams that paint a picture of his destiny (vv.5-11). One is of leadership over his family. The second indicates that he will rise above even his father in prominence and authority. With youthful zeal and immaturity, Joseph shares these things with his family, creating more conflict and further entrenching his brothers' hatred of him.

This hostility will soon spark a sequence of events—betrayal, slavery, false accusations, and broken promises, to name a few—that must make Joseph feel like the destiny foreshadowed by the robe and foreseen in his dreams is impossible.

But destiny does not happen in a day.

We all hold within our heart the sense of a dream, a vision of a preferred future. The journey from conception to consummation is never a straight line but one of seasons: There are bright summer days and 'long dark nights of the soul,' springtime growth and autumn fade. At times, we wonder where God is. *How can He possibly weave all of these threads together for our good and for His glory?*

Joseph's story reveals the answer to such questions. Although there is a long wait between the gift of the dreams and their fulfilment, Joseph remains faithful in each and every season. It becomes evident that his ability to maintain a steady course is because of his greater vision of the sovereignty of God; Joseph lives with an overwhelming sense that if God has given him a divine destiny, then no betrayal or adversity can deter Him from bringing about His will. Our vision and knowledge of God is what sustains us and stabilizes us whatever life throws our way, keeping us fixed on the truth that, like Joseph, our destiny is tied into a bigger story—the story God is writing across generations.

What is your own vision of God? As you think on the things you know to be true about Him, choose one attribute to focus your worship on today.

Prevailing Purpose

MAZHAR KEFALI

Genesis 38

"We interrupt this story to bring you breaking news!"

We're just beginning to become absorbed in Joseph's story when we encounter a very strange episode that has us wondering: *What's this got to do with Joseph?* But what feels like an interruption actually plays a pivotal role in advancing key themes in both Joseph's story and Genesis as a whole: God's sovereign grace and His prevailing purpose.

Judah, Jacob's fourth-born son, has moved away to stay with a man named Hirah from Adullam in Canaanite country, living amongst a people and culture that his family considers unclean. This occurs "at that time" when Joseph is sold into slavery (Genesis 37:36). Judah is the one who initiated the idea of selling Joseph; now he has fled. In this new land, he marries a Canaanite woman and has three sons: Er, Onan, and Shēlāh. When Er reaches the age of marriage, he is married to a woman named Tamar. And it is here that the story becomes perplexing.

Er is so wicked that God "put him to death" (Genesis 38:7). We're not told exactly what he's done, but the language conveys that it is so displeasing to God it demands his life. With his death, the levirate law kicks in. In the culture of the day, the continuation of the bloodline was of highest priority, so the custom was for the next brother in line to marry his brother's widow and supply an heir who would be considered the late brother's offspring.

Onan is the next brother in line. Knowing what the custom means, that the son born from his marriage to Tamar will not be seen as his own and will become Judah's heir, Onan chooses not to fulfil his duty—repeatedly (v.9). So the Lord put him to death also.

The third son, Shēlāh, is too young to marry at this point, so Tamar moves back into her father's home. Once Shēlāh reaches the age for marriage, however, Judah decides not to carry through with the custom in fear of his third son also dying. Upon realising this, Tamar devises a plan to seduce Judah so she will conceive. As scandalous as this sounds to us, according to the law of the day, it was a legitimate course of action; if the sons died and couldn't carry out the levirate law, then it could fall to the father-in-law.

But Judah will not willingly fulfil his duty. So Tamar dresses as a prostitute, propositions Judah, and becomes pregnant with twins, tricking him into giving her his seal and staff so that she can later confirm his identity as their father. Once he learns of Tamar's pregnancy and is confronted with the truth of whose children she's carrying, Judah acknowledges her as being "more righteous than I" (v.26). The idea of this phrase is 'to be right, just, justified, in the right with a just cause.' He knows that Tamar has acted righteously to ensure an heir for his household, whereas he has acted faithlessly in not allowing her to marry Shēlāh.

In all the scandal of this story, we see that God is preserving the seed of Jacob and the Messianic line; the sinfulness of man cannot hinder His sovereign plan. One of the twins, Perez, will become the ancestor of David (Ruth 4:18), and David, the ancestor of Jesus Christ (Matthew 1:3). In this preservation, we also see the riches of God's grace and mercy: Tamar will be honoured for her righteousness, featuring in the ancestral and Messianic line of Christ , her name becoming synonymous with blessing (Ruth 4:12) , and Judah, despite his sin, will head a royal line from whom "the scepter will not depart" (Genesis 49:10).

As we look at our own lives, the story of Tamar and Judah reminds us that neither our circumstances nor sinful choices—our own or others'—can thwart God's plans. His Word never returns empty but always accomplishes what He desires and achieves the purposes for which He sent it (Isaiah 55:11).

What promise or purpose of God feels like an impossibility in your life or family line? Declare Isaiah 55:11 over that situation and thank God for His power already at work in your circumstances.

Birds and Nests

MAZHAR KEFALI

Genesis 39

Martin Luther once famously said, "You cannot stop the birds from flying over your head, but you can stop them from building a nest there," meaning that temptations cannot be avoided, but we can choose our response to them. And as we rejoin Joseph in Genesis 39, we find a rather large bird circling his head, looking for a place to land.

Joseph has risen to prominence in Potiphar's house. Potiphar is a man of great power and influence; as the captain of the guard, he leads the men who protect Pharaoh and is the chief executioner—not a man you would want to cross. However, Joseph has gained great favour with Potiphar, who has noticed that the Lord is with Joseph and everything he touches seems to prosper. As a result, he has been put in charge of all Potiphar's affairs, becoming his personal attendant and second in command.

All seems to be going well for Joseph until he catches the attention of Potiphar's wife, who notices that Joseph is "well-built and handsome" (v.6) and "cast(s) longing eyes" on him (v.7 NKJV). In a not-so-subtle moment, she directly invites him into her bed! Joseph's response is a profound lesson in resisting temptation.

Joseph has chosen to live for an audience of one. He knows that God is not only sovereign, but all-knowing (Psalm 139); that all of life is lived in His presence and all sin is ultimately an offense against Him. So when presented with the opportunity to lie with his master's wife, his response is, "How could I do such a wicked thing and sin against God?" (v.9). Joseph understands that not only would such a course of action damage his relationship with his master, it would damage his relationship with God.

This creates a second response: the fear of the Lord. In Genesis 42:18, Joseph declares that he fears God, and it is this heart-attitude that causes him to never want to offend God. Every form of temptation reveals the disposition of our heart: *Do we desire to honour the Lord or to flirt with temptation?* A healthy 'fear' of God is a deterrent from sinning (Exodus 20:20) and opens us to the wisdom of God, giving us the ability to choose what is right when under pressure (Proverbs 1:7; 9:10).

These two guiding principles cause Joseph to maintain a life of integrity and purity. Someone once defined integrity as "the quality of character that chooses to not violate or defile one's identity and value." When we realise who we are as God's beloved children, understanding our identity in Christ, we will desire to not violate that. We will also find ourselves not wanting to violate that in others, as is seen in Joseph's respect for his master. Knowing we are loved, valued, and His motivates us to want to live a pure life in His eyes (1 John 3:1-3).

All of these characteristics and beliefs enable Joseph to refuse to give in to sin, even though such a stand costs him dearly when Potiphar's wife falsely accuses him of trying to rape her. The penalty of the day was death, but it is apparent that Potiphar knows the truth about his wife, and out of respect for Joseph, he places him in prison instead. But if Joseph is going to be a prisoner, he is going to be the best one! And so even there, we see the favour of God upon him, and Joseph once again finds himself promoted.

No matter what circumstances Joseph finds himself in, he chooses to serve God and those in authority above him regardless of the cost to himself. Neither temptation nor adversity are able to corrupt him because he has determined in advance who his allegiance belongs to and holds to it with great integrity. And we must, too.

Is there any way in which you are 'flirting with temptation'? What boundaries might you need to put in place in order to guard your heart and honour God?

Proven True

MAZHAR KEFALI

Genesis 40

Great promises, great callings require great preparation of a person's character in order to have the capacity to carry them out. Such is the journey of Joseph. God shapes him through adversity, using his time in slavery and prison to prepare him for his destiny. The pride and self-sufficiency that brought him so much trouble in his youth are replaced by dependence upon God, and because of this, it is evident to everyone who interacts with Joseph that God is with him—both in his suffering and his successes.

After several years in prison, two key figures in the palace, the cupbearer and the baker, offend Pharoah in such a manner that he throws them into prison, where they are placed under the care of Joseph. Some time later, each of them has a dream through which God reveals to them their future. But neither understand their dreams.

As the cupbearer and baker interact with Joseph the following day, we see that God has used Joseph's suffering to form in him great empathy. He notices that these men look "dejected" and "sad" (vv.6-7) and reaches out to them, inviting them to tell him their dreams. The chief cupbearer recounts his first, and Joseph tells him the meaning: He will be reinstated to his former position. Upon hearing this, the chief baker shares his dream. Unfortunately, this time the interpretation is not so favourable: His life will end in execution as opposed to promotion.

On his birthday, Pharoah reinstates the chief cupbearer and executes the chief baker, fulfilling the interpretations of the dreams. Joseph had made one request of the chief cupbearer, asking that, upon his release, he "remember" Joseph and "show him kindness" by telling Pharoah about his unjust situation. But the cupbearer forgets him.

By the time the cupbearer does remember him (Genesis 41:9), Joseph has been in prison for approximately ten years and a slave for three before that. But even as he has continued to serve God and others with an honourable, trusting heart throughout his trials, there is still the desire for justice for every unjust and unfair action against him (Genesis 40:15).

In Psalm 105, we gain insight into God's dealings with Joseph during his imprisonment (vv.16-22). Verse 19 sums it up well: God is working to bring about what He "foretold" and that His word will "prove him [Joseph] true." The phrase "proved him true" conveys the idea of being refined, as with the testing of metals to prove their genuineness and purity. God had sent Joseph ahead, positioning him to be ready to lead a nation through turbulent times. Through adversity, God tests and shapes Joseph to be proven true for this task. Joseph passes the test, and in every obstacle he faces, he retains his integrity and trust in God. No one and nothing can take away his faith in the sovereignty and trustworthiness of God.

It is natural for the human heart to wonder where God is and why it is taking so long for His promises to be outworked. But God is in no hurry as He prepares people for His purposes, as is seen in the lives of so many figures like Joseph within Scripture—Abraham, Moses, David, Paul, and even Christ. In times of waiting, God is testing our hearts (Deuteronomy 8:1-3); forging in us what is needed for our own assignments. But ultimately, God is foremostly concerned with shaping us into the image of Christ. When we face trials and delays, we can rejoice in how they help to conform us to His likeness, proving the genuineness of our faith which is of greater worth than gold (1 Peter 1:6-7).

What trial is God inviting you to rejoice in? How is the Father using this circumstance to lovingly shape you more and more into the image of Christ? Thank Him for His work in your life.

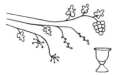

The Right Key

ELLIE DI JULIO

Genesis 41:1-36

There are over a dozen keys on my keychain. Most are house keys, some to doors I haven't stepped through in years, and they basically all look the same. And because I have no idea which one goes to what door, I'm constantly fumbling to match them up. I make my best guess and try each one until I get it right. Some won't go in at all; some do, but grind; some slide in effortlessly, but don't turn. There's only one key that will unlock the door I'm trying to get through.

Joseph has no doubt done a lot of thinking about doors and locks and keys by the time Pharaoh calls him up from prison. He's been three years behind bars and over a decade in slavery. After spending half his life in bondage, Joseph is undoubtedly ready to be free.

Unfortunately, freedom isn't what troubled Pharaoh has in mind. As Joseph steps into the throne room, he finds himself presented with yet another set of dreams to decipher. He takes a breath, nervously runs a hand over his freshly-shorn head, and speaks.

And this time he does it right.

Not like the first time, when he bragged to his brothers and father about one day being so great they'd bow to him, taking all the credit for his vision without once mentioning God (Genesis 37:5-11).

Not like the second time when he gave the Lord only passing credit for his talent to correctly interpret the cupbearer's and baker's dreams (Genesis 40:8-19).

No—this time, when Pharaoh calls on him, Joseph humbly denies any natural talent for divination, giving full and entire credit to God not just once but *five* times (Genesis 41:16, 25, 28, 32 & 34).

The first time Joseph spoke about dreams landed him in chains. The second time kept him there. But by relinquishing his ego to give God the glory He deserves, the third time he speaks about dreams, he receives not just his freedom but all the promises of his very first ones (Genesis 41:39-45; 42:6).

After thirteen years of fumbling, Joseph finally puts the right key—his gift of prophetic vision—in the right lock—fully submitting it to God—and opens the door to the blessing the Lord has had prepared all along. A blessing that spills over from him to his family to the nations of Egypt and Israel to believers and unbelievers alike.

The Lord has given each of us dreams and gifts, designed to be used for His Kingdom and His glory, for the good of all His children. But it's easy for them to get lost in our metaphorical keychain. We often try to use our key in the wrong lock or to force open doors not meant for us. And then we wonder why we aren't progressing towards the vision God gave us for our lives.

There is only one key to unlocking the door of blessing we're trying to get through: submitting to the will and the way of God. When our gifts are used more for our glory than God's, they can't take us into the great blessing waiting on the other side of the door of submission. It's only by balancing confidence in what He's given us with the humility to yield to Him that we can unlock our full purpose. That's the key.

What gifts or callings do you need to submit to the Lord? How do you sense He is inviting you to steward them for His glory in this season?

Winter Seasons

SHELLEY JOHNSON

Genesis 41:37-57

The winter dragged long though the days were short. In the grips of illness and loneliness, my joy plummeted with the temperatures. Smothered by dreariness and disease, the temptation to despair rose within me. *When would God answer my prayers?*

Winter seasons of our soul can cause us to question God's presence and goodness. We wonder if He really sees us and if He truly rescues and redeems—then we read a story like Joseph's and are encouraged to believe God for what He has promised. We begin to see that, for all our losses, there is much that God gives.

After years of slavery and wrongful imprisonment, Joseph's long winter finally blooms with new life when Pharaoh likes his plan for storing up grain during the years of plenty (Genesis 41:39-40). As a display of favour, Pharaoh lavishes abundant compensation on him, leaving for us an account of how much has been given to Joseph, a man whose life and everything in it had once been taken.

Pharaoh, so affected by Joseph's discerning spirit, puts the former Hebrew slave in charge over Egypt, making him the second-in-command of all the land. As a sign of this elevated status, Joseph receives a signet ring, fine robes, and a gold chain—symbols of power and authority. To further make the people aware of Joseph's new position, Pharaoh commands a chariot ride through the streets of Egypt, which gives Joseph the respect due his new station. He repeatedly emphasizes his elevation of Joseph to demonstrate to his officials that the decision is final.

The blessings continue to be poured out when Joseph is given both a new name and the daughter of a prince as his wife. Standing in stark juxtaposition to his thirteen years of slavery and imprisonment—seasons where no one knew his name nor claimed him as their own—these gifts exemplify Joseph's new season of abundance.

Stepping out of the darkness of his long winter, Joseph establishes himself in his new role, traveling across the country to store up food throughout the seven years of bounty (vv.46-48). The one who has been given much now becomes the giver. Never taking advantage of his station or power, Joseph hands out rations of grain to all who come to him for food—even people of other nations (v.57). Joseph proves trustworthy with everything he's been given.

When his wife, Potephera, gives him two sons, the favour of faithful Joseph multiplies. Aptly, his son's names capture the essence of his life's journey. Manasseh's name, meaning 'forgetfulness,' becomes a reminder of how far God has brought Joseph, blessing him with the ability to *forget* the suffering he's endured for thirteen years, while Ephraim's name, meaning 'fruitful,' captures the beauty of Joseph's new, bountiful season. And Joseph gives God all the credit.

For all the injustice Joseph has borne, he is met with rewards exceedingly beyond anything he could have asked or imagined (Ephesians 3:20). Through the riches and honour he is accorded, we see that his patient perseverance comes to a fruitful end. His trust in God pays off, and we come away from Joseph's story with assurance that God is faithful, even in seasons of loss and suffering. We can step into life with a stronger faith that no matter the season, God is good; He never leaves us nor forsakes us (Isaiah 41:10). And, like Joseph, we can trust that God will give us everything we need to flourish in the hard and the good.

Which of nature's seasons most reflects your current season of life: winter, spring, summer, or autumn? Reflect on its rhythm and ask God what He means to teach you by it.

Grains of Hope
RACHEL LOUISE

Genesis 42

As famine sweeps over the land, Jacob hears of grain in Egypt. The Hebrew word here for 'grain,' *shever*, is interchangeably read as *sever*, meaning 'hope.' Jacob looks towards Egypt and sees hope. But awaiting him there is something even greater than grain to ward off starvation: The road to Egypt is also the road to Joseph, his beloved son who, against all odds, is alive.

As Jacob's sons travel to Egypt in the hope of securing provision, Benjamin (meaning 'the son of my right hand') in many ways symbolises Christ. Like Jesus, he represents both the blameless one and the most beloved son (1 Peter 2:22; Matthew 17:5); he is the one through which the family's hope may be fulfilled, just as our greatest hopes are fulfilled in Christ (1 Peter 1:3).

Unrecognised by his brothers, Joseph seeks to test them, asking that they return with Benjamin so their brother Simeon may be released (v.19-20). Reuben sees this as retribution for their violence against Joseph and that "now they must give an accounting for his blood" (v.22). The sacrifice of putting innocent Benjamin in harm's way, even to obtain grain and set Simeon free from prison, is too high a price. Jacob forbids his most favoured remaining son to go (v.38).

In a narrative utterly shot through with the person of Christ, chapter 42 ends with this finality. We are left in a bleak 'not yet' where the required sacrifice is withheld. Christ has not yet come. Here, we so clearly see ourselves.

We are Simeon, held captive by our sin until the Blameless One arrives.

We are Reuben, painfully aware that our wrongdoings need accounting for.

We are Jacob's household, on the road to death unless the most Beloved Son is sacrificed.

But, oh, how much sweeter our story ends.

Our Heavenly Father *has* let His only Beloved Son go. And like grain beaten on the threshing floor to make flour for bread, Christ's body was broken as He became our Bread of Life that we may have life that outlasts death and carries us into eternity (John 6:35). Christ is the Hope we are set on pilgrimage towards, the One through whom our guilt is removed. And as we make our way towards Him, we ever more clearly see the character of God.

Under the weight of their guilt, Jacob and his sons endure a distorted view of reality. In being given back their silver along with the grain, the brothers tremble, asking, "What is it that God has done to us?" (v.28). They see a merciful act as a plot to enslave them. They are terrified by kindness. They are unable to accept grace.

In Christ, we receive freely, knowing we are undeserving. Yet in coming to remove our guilt, Christ calls us to enjoy rather than fear His kindness.

Hemmed in by the loss of Joseph and the danger looming over Benjamin and Simeon, Jacob concludes, "Everything is against me!" (v.36). Awash in grief and fear, he is unable to see beyond the acquisition of grain to the reconciliation of his family and the miraculous return of Joseph. Chest-deep in brokenness, Jacob cannot yet rise above his circumstances far enough to trust that God is working *for* him.

In Christ, we have fresh perspective. We are set free to see and know that "in all things God works for the good of those who love him, who have been called according to his purpose" (Romans 8:28).

May our eyes be open to receiving the hope of Christ, our Bread of Life, today. To see that God has given freely of Himself in merciful kindness, and that, when all things appear against us, He is truly working for our good, that in Him alone, we may live and not die (Psalm 118:17).

How have guilt and condemnation stood in the way of you freely receiving God's grace? Take a moment to pray over these things, surrendering them to Christ, and ask Him to give you a fresh perspective.

Abundant Grace

SINA STEELE

Genesis 43

As a new Christian in my early twenties, I spent hours poring over my Bible, fascinated by the stories that lay within. I had encountered the extravagant grace of God in my life, and I was hungry to know more. One story in particular that struck a chord with me was that of Joseph and how he comes face-to-face with his brothers after many years apart. I remember reading through tears as he prepares a meal for them—the same brothers who had betrayed him by selling him into slavery all those years earlier: "Joseph hurried out for he was deeply stirred over his brother, and he sought a place to weep; and he entered his chamber and wept there" (Genesis 43:30).

Here is this man, a Hebrew leader among the Egyptians, utterly undone by seeing his youngest brother. I cried when I read this, imagining the sorrow, homesickness, grief, and loneliness that he likely carried all those years in a foreign land, far from home. I imagined how it must have felt to see Benjamin standing before him, his only full brother, living the life he should be living, had he not been betrayed.

Yet Joseph comports himself with humility and treats his brothers with kindness. He is a strong and powerful man, yet gentle enough to allow himself to feel the deep emotions that stir within. Seeing his brothers evokes such a depth of feeling and memories buried within.

Once Joseph is able to compose himself from weeping, he puts on a feast for his guests—in the midst of a huge famine. Unsurprisingly, his brothers are fearful, wondering why such a demonstration of unmerited kindness. Later, when they discover who Joseph really is, they will come to understand the extent of that grace. Joseph is not angry, for he understands that God has a plan which He will outwork, even through the sinfulness of man (a fact which becomes evident in subsequent chapters of Joseph's story). Joseph's brothers would have been content with a simple meal, or even nothing at all, yet through Joseph, God is beginning to show them His abundant grace—giving above and beyond to those who feel they are in debt.

This is a beautiful foreshadowing of Jesus and how He treats us—not as our sins deserve but with grace, revealing His character in the process. Joseph's brothers don't deserve the kindness extended to them by their brother. They betrayed him by selling him into slavery, yet he still demonstrates love towards them. And so it is with Jesus. He knows mankind is full of sin, yet He went to the Cross, choosing suffering and a life of yielding to God's plan, for our redemption.

Just like Jesus, Joseph does not focus on the past failures of others but has a heart of compassion and forgiveness towards them. How precious and how redemptive this moment is. I think that's why I cried the first time I read Joseph's story, having just experienced the redeeming power of Christ in my own life. And the truth is, years later, He is still redeeming my story. But what's incredible about this point in the narrative is that Joseph's identity has not yet been revealed to his brothers. They have shown no repentance or remorse for their original betrayal of Joseph, and yet, for conscience's sake before God, he treats them with mercy, forgiveness, and love. Joseph's compassion for his brothers reveals to us a glimpse of God's character—abounding in compassion and full of extravagant grace.

Think back to when you first encountered the abundance of God's grace toward you. How did this change the trajectory of your life? Take a moment to thank God for His kindness.

The Best-laid Plans

JEFF MCKEE

Genesis 44

Joseph is doing okay. From prison he had been catapulted into power, glory, and honour. On the home front, he now has a wife and a couple of children. Even what he named his two boys is a testament to him being in a better place—God has made him forget his troubles and made him fruitful (Genesis 41:51-52).

In short, Joseph has made a new life. The past is in the past—at least, until he sees his brothers queuing for food. Recognising them immediately, he needs a plan. *What is he to do with them?* Joseph's first thoughts are: *They are responsible for the pain I endured. I don't need anything from them. They don't even need to know who I am!*

But then he gets curious. Without revealing himself, the brothers and Joseph talk about their family back in Canaan, and faint desire sparks in Joseph's heart. He needs time to think. Unfortunately, his first response proceeds from his past pain: The long-time prisoner promptly throws his brothers into jail.

Meanwhile, Joseph devises Plan B: *My mother is dead, and Benjamin is all I have left in terms of real family. I must see him . . . and I know how to get this done.*

Leaving Simeon in prison as a hostage, Joseph demands they bring Benjamin to him (Genesis 42:19-20). The plan works. Eventually they arrive in Egypt with the boy. It's the middle of a famine, but such is Joseph's exaltation in seeing his brother that Benjamin is offered five times the helpings of the others as they eat together.

As the eleven of them depart, Joseph feels an unexpected sense of loss. His heart aches until he realises that his past still has something to offer. Benjamin is his flesh and blood—and he wants him for keeps!

Yet again he is dissatisfied with the outcome, so In the intervening months, Joseph contrives plan C:

Who knows what will happen to Benjamin after my father dies? I will frame him for theft, then seize him. My other brothers care nothing for Rachel's children. They will probably be grateful to see the back of him, and Benjamin can share my good fortune here in Egypt. It's best for the both of us.

Again, Joseph's pain is speaking. As a boy he had been framed and seized— now he's projecting his hurt onto someone he truly loves.

Sure enough, the brothers return. Soon the trap is laid and Benjamin is caught apparently red-handed. He has the stolen goods! Joseph is poised to take Benjamin captive, but in a sudden redemptive moment, he and his plot are thrown into tatters. As Judah speaks up, Joseph discovers the full extent of Jacob's heart for him and for Benjamin, and that Judah loves his father and the boy just as he does. Joseph hadn't banked on that. As he witnesses this love, something shifts in Joseph. *Maybe these brothers who have done him so much wrong, have, in fact, changed.*

With a lighter heart, Joseph embraces a different plan, *a divine plan*—one that will result in the saving of his family and his people (Genesis 46:31-34). In doing so, he will discover that this was God's intention for him all along: He would gather his family to his adopted country for preservation there until centuries later they would grow into a nation, ready to set out and possess the Promised Land.

We are all a little like Joseph. It is easy to be shaped by pain in a way that corrupts our closest relationships and hinders God's will in our lives. Maybe we think we are doing okay, content to leave the past in the past. But God wants more for us than just 'moving on.' His extravagant gospel allows us to let go of our pain, discover our significance in God's greater purposes, and step confidently into the destiny He has for us.

God's plans are seldom our plans; they are infinitely better. As you lay aside your own understanding, what redemptive thing is God doing in and around you that could be a doorway into healing and His future for you?

The Great Why

JENNA MARIE MASTERS

Genesis 45

Joseph was hated by his brothers, betrayed and beaten, thrown in a pit, sold into slavery, falsely accused of rape, and thrown into jail. *And for what?* I wonder if he dragged the haunting question to God: *Why?*

All humans struggle with this burden. In our family, we have pursued adoption for eight years, and every effort has failed. Believe me, "The Great Why" has ricocheted off our walls: *Why did you put a desire in our hearts and then withhold it? Why did you let us lose twenty thousand dollars in this process? Why did you allow us to take a baby home, knowing he wouldn't stay with us?*

There are times when I imagine what I'd like to say to those who crushed our spirits, times I wanted to sue people and send raging letters. But suffering can make us either bitter or beautiful; hardships can be an opportunity to become more like Jesus. Romans tells us our suffering produces hope and that "hope does not put us to shame, because God's love has been poured out into our hearts through the Holy Spirit" (5:3). The Holy Spirit longs to fill us up so that, like Christ, His love overflows to those around us—even our enemies.

Joseph powerfully demonstrates this, having every right to consider his brothers his enemies. He could have thrown them in jail or worse; instead, he forgives them, gifting them silver, fine clothes, provisions, and the best land in Egypt. He kisses them, weeping, saying, *"Come close to me. Do not be distressed. I will provide for you. I will save your lives by a great deliverance"* (vv.4-11).

He sounds so much like our Saviour; it's astounding. Saving grace has become more important than saving face. Jesus, betrayed, handed over to authorities, beaten, humiliated, and hung on a cross to die, had the authority to bring judgment on everyone involved, but instead He prayed, "Father, forgive them, for they do not know what they are doing" (Luke 23:34). As men drove nails into His flesh, the urgent need to love them rushed to the surface above all else.

Jesus suffered all this to call us sons and daughters. And there I was, lamenting our few failed adoptions when God has thousands reject Him as

Father every day. We may question the purpose of our suffering, but Jesus never questioned His. Instead, He chose to walk in the way of love, giving Himself up for us (Ephesians 5:2).

A few years ago, I found myself sharing our adoption journey with a woman I'd just met. Wide-eyed, she interrupted me, "Five years?! How have you had the strength to go through all this and keep going?!" I knew nothing about her relationship with God, but she was shifting her weight side to side, waiting for my answer, so I gave her an honest one, "God. It's only through God."

Sometimes, I expect everyone to revolve around me because I'm hurting. But perhaps the overwhelming paperwork, financial sacrifice, nights sobbing on the bathroom floor, the naming and un-naming of children I thought were ours was all to testify to *one* woman that God is strong enough to sustain us through our suffering. *Would that be enough for me? Do I have the heart of Jesus to suffer in order to love* one *person?*

God's heart is missional. Joseph understands this. He has suffered, God has saved Him, and in turn, he wants to save others. Instead of hardening my heart towards people who cause me pain, Jesus reminds me that He hung on the Cross for *them*, too. We may not get an answer to every *why* this side of Heaven, but we can view our difficulties not only as a path to intimacy with our Saviour but also as a branch of salvation we can offer to others.

Consider your own 'Great Why'. How might God be inviting you to allow that place of suffering to be used for His redemptive purposes and to minister to others?

Not of This World

AMBER PALMER

Genesis 46

An image of a mouldy pear stopped me in my tracks as I was scrolling through my social media feed one morning—it was surrounded by other fruit that had also started to mould in the areas nearest to the rotting fruit. The caption mentioned how easily we start to become like the things we are closest to, and I was struck by how this is also true spiritually. It's all too easy for the bad things of the world to corrupt us—sometimes without us even noticing it. We can think we've kept enough distance between us and evil, but if we're not careful, just like that fruit, our hearts slowly become 'spoiled.' That morning, my mindless scrolling became a reminder of the importance of being in this world but not of it.

At the end of Genesis 46, Jacob and his family leave their home in Canaan to settle in Egypt—a land saturated in idolatry and pagan gods. Although Egypt appears to be the last place Jacob should be uprooting his family to, God assures him in a vision that this is where He has called him to be and promises to be with him and protect him (vv.3-4). So Jacob gathers all of his family and possessions to travel to Egypt and be with Joseph.

When they are finally reunited, Joseph prepares his father for a meeting with Pharaoh, telling Jacob he must say he has been a shepherd since his youth. *Why would he want them to emphasise that they are the very thing Egyptians loathe—shepherds?* Like that rotten pear that had polluted the rest of the fruit bowl, Joseph is well aware of the danger the temptations of Egypt pose. He knows if Pharaoh knows their occupation, he will require Jacob's family to live in Goshen: a fertile land situated on the outskirts of Egypt whose name means 'to draw near.' This place will not only allow them to thrive during the famine, it will also protect them from absorbing Egyptian culture. God uses the very thing that should cause them to be ostracised to protect them from being drawn into ungodly practices and to enable them to keep drawing near to Him, the one true God.

Until we leave our earthly dwelling for our eternal home, we will be in this world. We can't hide until the Lord returns. That means we have to make choices about what we live close to. We have to be careful to "strip off and throw aside every encumbrance (unnecessary weight) and that sin which so readily (deftly and cleverly) clings to and entangles us" and to be intentional about renewing our hearts and habits daily so we can "run with patient endurance and steady and active persistence the appointed course of the race that is set before us" (Hebrews 12:1 AMPC).

Just as God is with Jacob and the future Israelites, protecting them from assimilation into Egyptian customs, He is also with us. We have been given the gift of the Holy Spirit to help us walk in this world but not be of it, guiding and prompting us to keep our eyes on Jesus and to guard our hearts. John 14:15-17 promises us that He will be with us forever and that we will know Him because He will live within us.

Whenever we feel on the outside, rejected and excluded, we can trust that God's hand of protection is over us, providing us with shelter as He shields us from absorbing the unspiritual mould growing around us. In turn, when we live in such a way that draws us nearer to God, others around us will experience Him through us. Our steadfast faith becomes the antidote to the unspiritual ways of the world, catching like wildfire and drawing others to Jesus.

What habits help keep your heart and eyes oriented on Jesus? How could you be more intentional with these in this season?

When the Flowers Fall

RACHEL LOUISE

Genesis 47

"I just really, *really* don't want to be flatting forever," I sighed to Mum over FaceTime, feeling my eyes well up. My time in my current flat, with these wonderful people, was coming to a close, and I was on the brink of a fresh, promising chapter with new wonderful people. But uncertainty was loud and looming. And it didn't feel great.

As a young twenty-something, my deep desire to cultivate a family and settle in a home of my own feels very much at odds with the reality of life; I long for a more permanent home, yet I've just signed my second one-year tenancy agreement. I know following Jesus sets our hearts on pilgrimage, but often my heart is set on finding a place to land.

As we find them in Genesis 47, the Israelites are also a people characterised as being on pilgrimage. When the land of Canaan enters a crippling famine, Joseph's family petitions Pharaoh to sojourn in Egypt; not to settle forever, but to dwell there until they may shepherd their own land again (v.4). They know the Lord has called them to Canaan and that they are ultimately called to a permanent home in the heavenly land (Hebrews 11:13-16).

Nearing the end of his life, Jacob has his sights set on this home. Having just settled in Egypt, he looks towards his final settling in the land of his fathers (v.29-30) and describes to Pharaoh his life of pilgrimage and difficulty (v.9). Despite his hardships, here in his final years, he sees great provision and God's faithfulness despite being in a strange land (v.12).

Through Joseph, the Lord has made a way to preserve life. He has drawn Abraham's line out of Canaan to fulfil His promise, but this preservation of life is also extended to those under Joseph's rule. The land and its people are withering away, but not without hope of renewal (v.19). Seeds are sown to replenish and nourish them both; seeds are sown in the hope of life. In the face of hardship, we aren't to throw up our hands in despair but to draw on the hope of Heaven and plant again, here and now.

Through Jesus, the Lord has made a way to preserve *eternal* life, as well. Christ, the Gardener of our hearts and souls, has sown seeds in His death that we may live and not die (John 11:25-26). So the joys and triumphs and beauty of our lives may be caught up in eternity. So that we may enter our forever home.

We might not feel entirely settled or at home in our own lives, but the Lord promises to meet our needs (Romans 8:32). We are told we will see trouble in this life of pilgrimage (John 16:33), but we will also see provision, blessing, and the fruit of God's faithfulness; even in days of famine, we are offered the promise of plenty (Psalm 37:19).

The seen reality of this new home I'm going to will fade. The sweet peas, carnations, and lilies we're planting will pass away. But in the unseen things, in the conversations and relationships, joy and hospitality, something enduring is sown. God is an everlasting being at work in a temporary world, making it into a new, eternal creation. He is doing deep work beyond what we can see. It is to this I hold—my hope: "The grass withers and the flowers fall, but the word of our God endures forever" (Isaiah 40:8).

How is God inviting you to sow into the place where you are presently planted? Even if it is a temporary landing place, ask the Spirit to keep your eyes and heart open to ways you can partner with Him to release the hope of Heaven there.

DAY FIFTY-EIGHT

Grief and Glory
JEFF MCKEE

Genesis 48

When news reached Jacob that his lost son, Joseph, was alive, he couldn't believe it. Perhaps he wandered out and sat on the well that would later be named for him; the one at Sychar that John would write about years later (John 4:12). We can't be sure, but we do know he took it on board. He made a firm decision to move to Egypt and accept Joseph's offer to live in Goshen's rich pastures (Genesis 46:3; 47:27).

I'm imagining the scene: He is packing, and it's not easy to move on. Suddenly he has a thought—when he set his affairs in order, he left Joseph out of the will, thinking his son was dead. Now he's found out his son is wondrously alive! *What should he do?* Sure, the inheritance can be split afresh to include one more, but that doesn't satisfy Jacob's heart. He wants to honour Joseph, just like when he once dressed the lad in a resplendent robe. *But how?*

The answer comes down to a matter of the heart.

Jacob had settled in Shechem. There he had enjoyed his happiest days, while Rachel was still living. Then, one tragedy followed another, and he left, only to return because this region truly is his own patch of the Promised Land. In a flash of inspiration, he has an idea! Sure, Joseph rules all Egypt—he belongs there now—but Jacob wants Rachel's eldest son to own a piece of his personal paradise. Jacob begins mulling over the purchase. *How will he pay for it?* That's when his sword and bow come to mind. *I won't be needing those where I'm going,* he thinks, and he sells them to make the purchase (Genesis 48:22).

With the title secured, he travels to Egypt to be reunited with his son at last. Along the way, he passes two places that remind him of earlier events in his life. The first is Bethel (Luz). There, in an encounter with God, all of the promises given to his father and grandfather had been affirmed in him as well (Genesis 35:11-12). No doubt the old man walks taller on the road after passing that spot. But then he comes to a place of much personal sorrow: In Bethlehem he had lost and buried the only woman he ever really loved (v.19). The memories there would have weighed him down, so we can easily picture him carrying both glory and grief as he passes through

Beersheba where he grew up, then continues down the long road towards his son.

Jacob arrives in Egypt and settles in, but he quickly weakens. Joseph hears that his father is dying and hurries to his bedside. The ancient man has many important things to say. Since arriving, there hasn't been nearly enough time to catch up on all the lost years. Now, as Jacob opens his mouth, all the glory and grief tumbles out, each vying for prominence in this significant moment (Genesis 48:3-16). Thankfully, the glory wins out! Laying aside his sorrow, Jacob's joy in the glorious spiritual inheritance God has released over him takes the lead. When Jacob sees his two grandchildren, he audaciously claims them as his own, positioning them to receive the glory in an undiluted way.

As we consider our children and grandchildren, our hearts and minds may also be awash with conflicting emotions. Our unmet expectations and broken dreams mean many of us have glory in one hand and grief in the other. Let's put one hand quietly behind our back and instead generously offer what's in the other to the generations ahead.

Where in your life has grief been the legacy you are carrying? How is God inviting you to instead carry and release His glory?

Blessing's Potential

JEFF MCKEE

Genesis 49

Jacob's last great act is one of blessing. Think about what this moment means to him after all his ambition and conniving to obtain his own blessing in the first place. Now we find him surrounded by a dozen grown sons, each eager to receive the priceless treasure of their father's powerful words of affirmation.

I didn't grow up knowing about blessings. We didn't talk about them; they just weren't on our radar. Also, our family was fractured on account of our parents' messy divorce. I still treasure what my brother, sister, and I received in terms of heritage—a love for Jesus and His Word and a lifestyle of sensitivity and obedience to His voice—but the foundations out of which a lavish spiritual inheritance could be passed on slowly crumbled before their time. That left me on the back foot as I tried to find my place in the world. I sometimes wonder, *what if....*

Jacob's sons are wondering, too. They know what this moment is about. For them and their children, grandchildren, and the whole Jewish race forever after, this moment is pivotal. They are full of anticipation, as well as misgivings. Some of them know, to their regret, Jacob's great sensitivity to their misdeeds; some of their actions are appalling to any person with a moral compass.

Perhaps this is why the first three 'blessings' read more like curses, ones that are apparently well-deserved. *Why?* They have done detestable things—incest on the one hand, and the mass slaughter of a whole community on the other (Genesis 34:25-30; 35:22). It seems a no-brainer that Jacob could have dealt with these issues within his family as they occurred—some combination of discipline and grace leading to repentance, restoration, and redemption—so that later, in this pivotal moment, he could have welcomed these three into blessing. The trouble is, he didn't, and now the clock has run down and this is their blessing day. In my mind, I think that there is still an opportunity for Jacob to rise above it all, regardless—to deal with their sin so his line can be the holy people God intended *and* offer them a father's blessing. But he doesn't, and devoid of this blessing, the trajectory of these three sons and their descendants becomes one of perpetual decline, so much so that in Deuteronomy, Moses will intercede for the tribe of Rueben to "live and not die" (33:6).

But as Jacob begins speaking over his fourth son, something changes. It's as if he gets totally airborne! There's a flow from Heaven—to the point that his words forge the throne of David and usher in the true Lion of Judah, even centuries later (Revelation 5:5)!

Every subsequent son is also blessed, and when he gets to Joseph, Jacob's spirit rises again, his insight reaching a whole other level as he bestows on him all of his own blessings (v.26). Jacob's words demonstrate blessing's potential to call out true identity and destiny—and what is lost when it is withheld.

Blessing requires the activation of the spirit—so we see more, understand more, and feel so much more; so we can speak with an authority and clarity that shapes futures and destinies around us. Yes, there will always be excuses to withhold affirmation and blessing. Our children may offend us, and our relationships can be strained, but the nature of blessing is to transcend circumstances and constraints. After all, when we bless, we are emulating Father God who lavishes favour on us in spite of literally everything.

I am convinced that we can outdo Jacob in blessing. The bitter sting of sin's curse was exacted on Christ as He suffered, leaving us better positioned to equip and empower the generations to follow. Passionately pursuing that is a critical investment in the future of the Kingdom of God on earth. We must lay aside judgement and ask ourselves the question: *What would I have loved to have spoken over me?* Then we can deliberately declare that, releasing it over our children's lives again and again

Like Jacob, we won't get it right every time, but a lifestyle of blessing can achieve what a moment may not. As parents who desire tremendous favour for our children and long for a full realisation of their potential, let us learn to rise in spirit and continually bless at every opportunity.

Where in your life do you need to rise above circumstance and emotion to express the Father's heart and release blessing?

God is the Constant

ASHLEY KELLY

Genesis 50

One of my Bible college teachers depicted the life of Joseph by drawing a line resembling hills and valleys on the whiteboard behind him. He then proceeded to illustrate the character of Joseph with one straight, horizontal line all the way through each hill and valley. Joseph's character is constant and consistent through every trial and every victory. This simple illustration is the only thing I distinctly remember from that class, and I think about it often.

This final chapter of Genesis poignantly ties a bow on the life of Joseph while also bringing into focus the character and nature of God. Over and over in Genesis, we have read about God's plan and promises, only to be faced with mankind's continual sin, shortcomings, and mistakes. But we are not left with a sense of despair or hopelessness. Rather, we are left with the bold, wise, and hopeful words of Joseph himself: "'You intended to harm me, but God intended it for good to accomplish what is now being done, the saving of many lives'" (v.20). This is a story of restoration and redemption, of God's absolute faithfulness. Ultimately, it is a story of our intentional God accomplishing what He wills—saving many lives—as He wills.

Joseph, a man of many trials, is able to reveal this truth about God because he first *lived it*. He did not read these words in a greeting card. He does not have Romans 8:28 in his back pocket, ready to pull out at this opportune time. You know the verse to which I'm referring: "And we know that in all things God works for the good of those who love him, who have been called according to his purpose." Generations and generations of ups and downs must still be lived through and recorded before Paul will pen these powerful words. For Joseph, though, nobody has to tell him God is at work, that God has a plan; he already knows that of God, believes it of him. Joseph is able to remain consistent through all the hills and valleys because all his life he has trusted and relied upon the faithfulness of God. Period.

Thousands of years later, we have the words of Joseph and Paul framed and hung on our walls. We send and receive greeting cards boasting their words. We encourage ourselves and others to remember God is working for good.

We memorise these verses, preach these verses, and sing these verses. *But do we live them? Do we stand in the valleys of pain and intended harm and refuse to give in or let go of our faith? Do we arrive on the hills of victory and intentionally glorify God above all else? Do we rely on mere words to get us through a tough situation, or do we turn our eyes and hearts upward, remembering and relying on who He is?*

Hills and valleys are an accurate way to describe more than just the life of Joseph. The story of Creation, mankind, the Flood, the patriarchs—the story that begins in Genesis and continues even now—is full of ups and downs, highs and lows. If we were to imagine it drawn out on a whiteboard, the one long, straight, horizontal line through it all would not be *our* character, but God's. God is the constant in all the chaos, the One who is not changed or swayed by the numerous hills and valleys. He is the One who remains faithful even if—*even when*—we are faithless (2 Timothy 2:13).

As we live convinced of God's consistent faithfulness and goodness, Joseph's words will become our words; we will become utterly convinced that God is always working for good—whatever He deems that is. And His good is always the best thing.

If you were to chart your own life's journey, what would it look like? How can you see the straight line of God's constancy and faithfulness throughout it?

CONTRIBUTING WRITERS

We are so grateful for our writing team and the heart and wisdom that they have brought to this project. Connect with them on Instagram, and read more of their work @thedevotedcollective.

Tristany Corgan	@tristanycorgan
Adéle Deysel	@adeledeysel
Ellie Di Julio	@elliedijulio
Shelley Johnson	@shelley.johnson.tx
Mazhar Kefali	@mazharkefali
Ashley Kelly	@rooted.and.strong
Rachel Louise	@shesrachelouise
Jenna Marie Masters	@marked_by_love
Anya McKee	@anyamckee
Jeff McKee	@jeffmckeenz
Paula Morrison	@paula_morrison2804
Nicole O'Meara	@nicoleeomeara
Amber Palmer	@myjarsofclay
Cara Ray	@pursuingotiumsanctum
Sina Steele	@sinasteele
Emily Tyler	@promiseseeker
Aimée Walker	@aimeerwalker

the DEVOTED Collective

Our vision is simple: to serve God with wholehearted devotion, fulfilling the command Christ gave us to love the Lord with all our heart, soul, and mind (Matthew 22:37).

We want to love God with all that we are, right where we are. In order to do that, The Devoted Collective is anchored in three core disciplines modelled for us in Acts 2:42: devotion to the Word, to community, and to prayer. It is our heart's desire that, through committing to these practices with us, you will experience the richness of all God intends for your life as you come to know Him more intimately.

The more we know God, the more we can't help but love Him; and the more we love Him, the more we'll desire to partner with Him to establish it on earth as it is in Heaven. And that's what wholehearted devotion is all about.

Connect with us on social media @thedevotedcollective

www.thedevotedcollective.org

CPSIA information can be obtained
at www.ICGtesting.com
Printed in the USA
BVHW060134210222
629616BV00003B/211

9 780473 613730